Introduction to
ATM Design and Performance

Introduction to ATM Design and Performance

With Applications Analysis Software

J M Pitts
J A Schormans

Queen Mary and Westfield College
University of London
UK

JOHN WILEY & SONS
Chichester • New York • Brisbane • Toronto • Singapore

Other Wiley Editorial Offices

John Wiley & Sons, Inc., 605 Third Avenue,
New York, NY 10158-0012, USA

Jacaranda Wiley Ltd, 33 Park Road, Milton,
Queensland 4064, Australia

John Wiley & Sons (Canada) Ltd, 22 Worcester Road,
Rexdale, Ontario M9W 1L1, Canada

John Wiley & Sons (Asia) Pte Ltd, 2 Clementi Loop #02-01,
Jin Xing Distripark, Singapore 0512

Library of Congress Cataloging-in-Publication Data

Pitts, J.M., Ph.D.
    Introduction to ATM design and performance : with applications analysis software
    / J.M. Pitts, J.A. Schormans.
        p.   cm.
    Includes bibliographical references and index.
    ISBN 0-471-96340-2
    1. Asynchronous transfer mode.   2. Telecommunication — Traffic.
    I. Schormans, J.A.   II. Title.
  TK5105.35.P57   1996
  621.3823 — dc20

                                                        96-5966
                                                        CIP

British Library Cataloguing in Publication Data

A catalogue record for this book is available from the British Library

ISBN 0 471 963402

Typeset in 10.5/12.5pt Palatino by Laser Words, Madras
Printed and bound in Great Britain by Bookcraft (Bath) Ltd.

This book is printed on acid-free paper responsibly manufactured from sustained forestation,
for which at least two trees are planted for each one used for paper production.

To
Suzanne, Rebekah and Verity
Jacqueline, Matthew and Daniel

Contents

Preface

In recent years, we have taught ATM design and performance evaluation techniques to undergraduates in the Department of Electronic Engineering at Queen Mary and Westfield College, and to graduates on the University of London M.Sc. courses in Telecommunications (URL: http://www.elec.qmw.ac.uk). We have found that many engineers and students of engineering experience difficulty in making sense of ATM issues and teletraffic techniques. This is partly because of the subject itself: ATM is flexible, complicated, and still evolving. However, some of the difficulties arise because of the advanced mathematical methods that have been applied to ATM analysis. The research literature, and many books reporting on it, is full of differing analytical approaches applied to a bewildering array of ATM traffic mixes, switch designs and traffic control mechanisms.

To counter this trend, our book, which is intended for use by students both at final year, undergraduate and postgraduate level, and by practising engineers in the telecommunications world, provides an *introduction* to ATM and its traffic issues. We cover performance evaluation by analysis and simulation, presenting key formulas describing traffic and queueing behaviour, and practical examples, with graphs and tables for the design of ATM networks.

In line with our general approach, derivations are included where they demonstrate an intuitively simple technique; alternatively we give the formula and then show how to apply it (as a bonus, all the formulas are available as Mathcad files, so there is no need to program them yourself). We have ensured that the need for prior knowledge (in particular, probability theory) has been kept to a minimum. We feel strongly that this enhances the work, both as a textbook and as a design guide, as it is far easier to make progress when you are not trying to deal with another subject in the background. Whilst we do not claim that the book is comprehensive, we do believe that it is understandable, and where appropriate we relate the fundamentals of ATM design to the latest versions of the evolving international standards.

Organisation

In Chapter 1, we describe ATM technology, highlighting the fundamental operation of ATM as it relates to performance issues, rather than describing the technology and standards in detail. Chapter 2 introduces the concept of resource sharing, which underpins the design and performance of any telecommunications technology, in the context of circuit switched networks. Here, we see the trade-off between the economics of providing telecommunications capability and satisfying the service requirements of the customer.

To evaluate the performance of shared resources, we need an understanding of queueing theory. In Chapter 3, we introduce the fundamental concept of a queue (or waiting line), its notation, and some elementary relationships, and apply these to the basic process of cell buffering in ATM. This familiarises the reader with the important performance measures of cell delay and cell loss, the typical orders of magnitude for these measures, and the use of approximations, *without* having to struggle through analytical derivations at the same time.

Chapter 4 describes a variety of simple traffic models, both for single sources and for aggregate traffic, with sample parameter values that are appropriate for ATM traffic sources. The distinction between different levels of traffic behaviour, particularly the cell and burst levels, is introduced, as well as the different ways in which timing information is presented in source models. Both these aspects are important in helping to simplify and clarify queueing analysis for ATM.

In Chapter 5, we treat the queueing behaviour of ATM cells in output buffers, taking the reader very carefully through the analytical derivation of the queue state probability distribution, the cell loss probability, and the cell delay distribution. The analytical approach used is a direct probabilistic technique which is simple and intuitive, and key stages in the derivation are illustrated graphically. This basic technique is the underlying analytical approach applied, in Chapter 11, to the more complex issues of priority mechanisms. In Chapter 5, we also show how end to end delay distributions are calculated.

Chapters 6 and 7 take the traffic models of Chapter 4 and the concept of different levels of traffic behaviour, and apply them to the analysis of ATM queueing. The distinction between cell scale queueing (Chapter 6) and burst scale queueing (Chapter 7) is of fundamental importance because it provides the basis for understanding and designing a traffic control framework (based on the international ATM standards) that can handle integrated, multi-service traffic mixes. This framework is described in Chapters 8, 9, 10 and 11. A key part of the treatment of cell and burst scale queueing is the use of explicit formulas, based on approximate analysis; these formulas can be rearranged for use in algorithms for connection admission control (Chapter 8), usage parameter control (Chapter 9), and buffer dimensioning (Chapter 10). In addition, Chapter 10 combines the cell and burst scale analysis with the connection level for link dimensioning, by incorporating Erlang's loss analysis introduced in Chapter 2. In Chapter 11, we build on the analytical approach, introduced in Chapter 5, to cover space and time priority issues. Finally, in Chapter 12, we introduce the fundamentals of simulation, and describe the basic principles of cell rate simulation, which is an accelerated technique modelling ATM at the burst level.

Acknowledgements

We would like to thank Professor Laurie Cuthbert and John Griffiths for their help and encouragement, and our families for their patience, understanding, and support.

Jonathan M. Pitts
John A. Schormans
London, March 1996

Applications Analysis Software

The diskette included with this book contains the following Mathcad™ files:

chap2.mcd   chap3.mcd   chap4.mcd   chap5.mcd   chap6.mcd
chap7.mcd   chap8.mcd   chap9.mcd   chap10.mcd   chap11.mcd
splash.mcu

There is one '.MCD' file for each of the chapters in the book containing analysis equations and graphs. To read these files you need to have Mathcad version 4.0 or later.

If you do not have Mathcad, but do have access to the World Wide Web, you can download the Mathcad Working Model from either of the following sites:

> http://www.mathsoft.com
> http://www.adeptscience.co.uk

This file, WRKMODEL.EXE, is a self-extracting compressed file. Run this file to extract various installation files, one of which is the SETUP.EXE program. Run SETUP.EXE to install the working model on your computer. Now copy SPLASH.MCU from the diskette included with this book into the HANDBOOK\MODEL directory created during installation of the working model. This modifies the Mathcad Working Model so that the first document you view contains all the equations and graphs from CHAP2.MCD up to CHAP11.MCD. Note that the links to the rest of the working model are maintained. You can change values, equations and graphs in the working model, but the one limitation is that you cannot save or print.

Feedback

If you have any comments or queries about the Mathcad files, please contact the publishers by email to:

> ahalliga@wiley.co.uk

or write to:

> Ann-Marie Halligan
> Publisher
> John Wiley & Sons Ltd.
> Baffins Lane
> Chichester
> West Sussex PO19 1UD
> UK

Trademarks

Mathcad is a registered trademark of MathSoft, Inc.

1 An Introduction to the Technology of ATM

the bare necessities

This chapter is intended as a brief introduction to the technology of the asynchronous transfer mode (ATM) on the assumption that you will need some background information before proceeding to the chapters on traffic engineering and design. If you already have a good working knowledge of ATM you may wish to skip this chapter, because we highlight the fundamental operation as it relates to performance issues rather than describe the technology and standards in detail. For anyone wanting a deeper insight we refer to [1] for a comprehensive introduction to the narrowband integrated services digital network (ISDN), and to [2] for a general introduction to ATM, including its implications for interworking and evolution.

1.1 CIRCUIT SWITCHING

In traditional analogue circuit switching, a call is set-up on the basis that it receives a path (from source to destination) that is its "property" for the duration of the call, i.e. the whole of the bandwidth of the circuit is available to the calling parties for the whole of the call. In a digital circuit switched system, the whole bit-rate of the line is assigned to a call for only a single time slot per frame. This is called time division multiplexing.

During the time period of a frame, the transmitting party will generate a fixed number of bits of digital data (for example, eight bits to represent the level of an analogue telephony signal) and these bits will be grouped together in the time slot allocated to that call. On a transmission link, the same time slot in every frame is assigned to a call for the duration of that call (Figure 1.1). So the time slot is identified by its position in the frame, hence use of the name "position multiplexing", although this term is not used as much as time division multiplexing.

When a connection is set up, a route is found through the network and that route remains fixed for the duration of the connection. The route will probably traverse a number of switching nodes and require the use of many transmission links to provide a circuit from source to destination. The time slot position used by a call is likely to be different on each link. The switches which interconnect the transmission links perform the time slot interchange (as well as the space switching) necessary to provide the "through-connection" (e.g. link M, time slot 2 switches to link N, time slot 7 in Figure 1.2).

In digital circuit switched telephony networks, frames have a repetition rate of 8000 frames per second (and so a duration of 125 μs), and as there are always eight bits (one byte) per time slot, each channel has a bit-rate of 64 kbit/s. With N time slots in each frame, the bit-rate of the line is N × 64 kbit/s. In practice, extra time slots or bits are added for control and synchronisation functions. So for example, the widely used 30 channel system has two extra time slots, giving a total of 32 time slots, and thus a bit-rate of $(30 + 2)64 = 2048$ kbit/s. Some readers may be more familiar with the 1544 kbit/s 24 channel system which has one extra bit per frame.

The time division multiplexing concept can be applied recursively by considering a 24 or 30 channel system as a single "channel", each frame of which occupies one time slot per frame of a higher order multiplexing

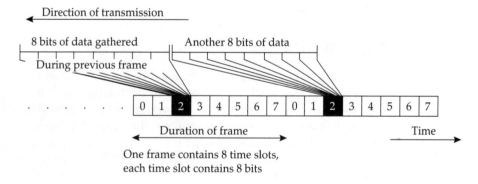

One frame contains 8 time slots,
each time slot contains 8 bits

Figure 1.1
An example of time division, or position, multiplexing

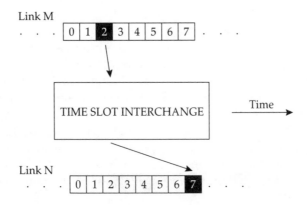

Figure 1.2
Time slot interchange

system. This is the underlying principle in the synchronous digital hierarchy (SDH), and an introduction to SDH can be found in [1].

The main performance issue for the user of a circuit switched network is whether, when a call is requested, there is a circuit available to the required destination. Once a circuit is established, the user has available a constant bit-rate with a fixed end-to-end delay. There is no error detection or correction provided by the network on the circuit — that's the responsibility of the terminals at either end, if it is required. Nor is there any per circuit overhead — the whole bit-rate of the circuit is available for user information.

1.2 PACKET SWITCHING

To see how ATM has evolved from both circuit switched and packet switched networks, it is helpful to consider a "generic" packet switching network, i.e. one intended to represent the main characteristics of packet switching, rather than any particular packet switching system.

Instead of being organised into single eight bit time slots which repeat at regular intervals, data in a packet switched network is organised into packets comprising many bytes of user data (bytes are also known as octets). Packets can vary in size depending on how much data there is to send, usually up to some predetermined limit (for example, 4096 octets). Each packet is then sent from switching node to node as a group of contiguous bits fully occupying the link bit-rate for the duration of the packet. If there is no packet to send, then nothing is sent on the link. When a packet is ready, and the link is idle, then the packet can be sent immediately. If the link is busy (another packet is currently being transmitted), then the packet must wait in a buffer until the previous one has completed transmission (Figure 1.3).

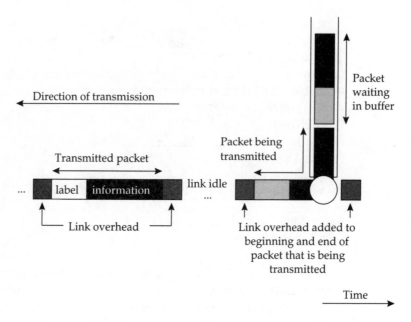

Figure 1.3
An example of label multiplexing

Each packet has a label to identify it as belonging to a particular communication. Thus packets from different sources and to different destinations can be multiplexed over the same link by being transmitted one after the other. This is called label multiplexing. The label is used at each node to select an outgoing link, routing the packet across the network. The outgoing link selected may be predetermined at the set-up of the connection, or it may be varied according to traffic conditions (e.g. take the least busy route). The former method ensures that packets arrive in the order in which they were sent, whereas the latter method requires the destination to be able to resequence out-of-order packets (in the event that the delays on alternative routes are different).

Whichever routing method is used, the packets destined for a particular link must be queued in the node prior to transmission. It is this queueing which introduces variable delay to the packets. A system of acknowledgments ensures that errored packets are not lost but are retransmitted. This is done on a link-by-link basis, rather than end-to-end, and contributes further to the variation in delay if a packet is corrupted and needs retransmission. There is quite a significant per packet overhead required for the error control and acknowledgment mechanisms, in addition to the label. This overhead reduces the effective bit-rate available for the transfer of user information. The packet plus link overhead is often (confusingly) called a "frame". Note that it is *not* the same as a frame in circuit switching.

A simple packet switched network may continue to accept packets without assessing whether it can cope with the extra traffic or not. Thus it appears to be non-blocking, in contrast to a circuit switched network which rejects (blocks) a connection request if there is no circuit available. The effect of this non-blocking operation is that packets experience greater and greater delays across the network, as the load on the network increases. As the load approaches the network capacity, the node buffers become full, and further incoming packets cannot be stored. This triggers retransmission of those packets which only worsens the situation by increasing the load; the successful throughput of packets decreases significantly.

In order to maintain throughput, congestion control techniques, particularly flow control, are used. Their aim is to limit the rate at which sources offer packets to the network. The flow control can be exercised on a link-by-link, or end-to-end basis. Thus a connection cannot be *guaranteed* any particular bit-rate: it is allowed to send packets to the network as and when it needs to, but if the network is congested then the network exerts control by restricting this rate of flow.

The main performance issues for a user of a packet switched network are the delay experienced on any connection and the throughput. The network operator aims to maximise throughput and limit the delay, even in the presence of congestion. Once a connection is established, the user is able to send information on demand. The network provides error control through re-transmission of packets on a link-by-link basis. Capacity is not dedicated to the connection, but shared on a dynamic basis with other connections. The capacity available to the user is reduced by the per packet overheads required for label multiplexing, flow and error control.

1.3 ATM AND THE CELL

So how does ATM combine circuit and packet switching? In very simple terms, the ATM concept maintains the time slotted nature of transmission in circuit switching (but without the position in a frame having any meaning) but increases the size of the data unit from one octet (byte) to 53 octets. Alternatively, you could say that ATM maintains the concept of a packet but restricts it to a fixed size of 53 octets, and requires packet synchronised transmission.

This group of 53 octets is called a cell. It contains 48 octets for user data — the information field — and 5 octets of overhead — the header. The header contains a label to identify it as belonging to a particular connection. So ATM uses label multiplexing and not position multiplexing. But what about the time slots? Well, these are called cell slots. An ATM link operates a sort of conveyor belt of cell slots (Figure 1.4). If

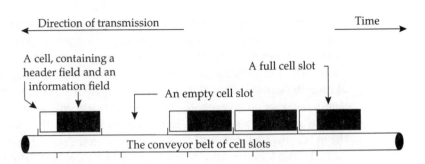

Figure 1.4
The conveyor belt of cells

there is a cell to send, then it must wait for the start of the next cell slot boundary — the next slot on the conveyor belt. The cell is not allowed to straddle two slots. If there is no cell to send, then the cell slot is unused, i.e. it is empty.

There is no need for the concept of a repeating frame, as in circuit switching, because the label in the header identifies the cell.

1.4   VIRTUAL CHANNELS AND VIRTUAL PATHS

Let's take a more detailed look at the cell header. The label consists of two components: the virtual channel identifier (VCI) and the virtual path identifier (VPI). These identifiers do not have end-to-end (user-to-user) significance; they identify a particular virtual channel (VC) or virtual path (VP) on the link over which the cell is being transmitted. When the cell arrives at the next node, the VCI and the VPI are used to look up in the routing table to which outgoing port the cell should be switched and what new VCI and VPI values the cell should have. The routing table values are established at the set-up of a connection, and remain constant for the duration of the connection, so the cells always take the same route through the network, and the "cell sequence integrity" of the connection is maintained.

But surely only one label is needed to achieve this cell routing mechanism, and that would also make the routing tables simpler: so why have two types of identifier? The reason is for the flexibility gained in handling connections. The basic equivalent to a circuit switched or packet switched connection in ATM is the virtual channel connection (VCC). This is established over a *series* of concatenated virtual channel links. A virtual path is a bundle of virtual channel links, i.e. it groups a number of VC links in *parallel*. This idea enables direct "logical" routes to be established between two switching nodes that are not connected by a direct physical link.

The best way to appreciate why this concept is so flexible is to consider an example. Figure 1.5 shows three switching nodes connected in a physical star structure to a "cross-connect" node. Over this physical network, a logical network of three virtual paths has been established. These VPs provide a logical mesh structure of virtual channel links between the switching nodes. The routing table in the cross-connect only deals with port numbers and VPIs — the VCI values are neither read, nor are they altered. However, the routing table in the switching nodes deal with all three: port numbers, VPIs and VCIs.

In setting up a VCC, the cross-connect is effectively invisible; it does not need to know about VCIs and is therefore not involved in the process. If there was only one type of identifier in the ATM cell header, then either direct physical links would be needed between each pair of switching nodes to create a mesh network, or another switching node would be required at the hub of the star network. This hub switching node would then have to be involved in every connection set-up on the network.

Thus the VP concept brings significant benefits by enabling flexible logical network structures to be created to suit the needs of the expected traffic flows. It is also much simpler to change the logical network structure than the physical structure. This can be done to reflect, for example, time-of-day changes in demand to different destinations.

In some respects the VP/VC concept is rather similar to having a two-level time division multiplexing hierarchy in a circuit switched network. It has extra advantages in that it is not bound by any particular framing structure, and so the capacity used by the VPs and VCs can be allocated in a very flexible manner.

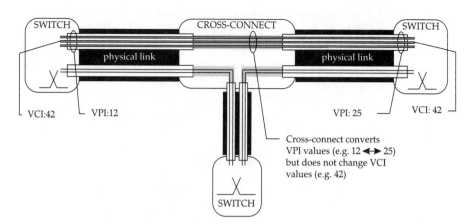

Figure 1.5
Virtual paths and virtual channels

1.5 MULTIPLEXORS, SWITCHES AND CROSS-CONNECTS

Nodes in a network handling ATM cells have to merge traffic streams from different sources and route them to different destinations via switch paths and transmission links which the cells share for part of their journey. This process involves the temporary storage of cells in finite sized buffers, the actual pattern of cell arrivals causing queues to grow and diminish in size. This is similar in principle to queueing in packet switched networks, although the speed of operation is significantly higher (typically 155.52 Mbit/s in ATM compared with 64 kbit/s for packet-switched networks).

A major difference, however, is the fact that there is no link-by-link acknowledgment and error control on the whole cell. The cell header is protected by an eight bit header error control (HEC) field. This is used to correct single-bit errors, and detect and discard cells with multiple errors. But there is no protection for the information field and no provision for cell retransmission over the link — if this is required it must be performed end-to-end by the terminals.

Thus the main job of multiplexors, switches and cross-connects is to provide temporary storage for cells in transit, and routing to the correct output port. We will see later that the study of queueing in these nodes is fundamental to the design, operation and performance of ATM networks. There is a great variety of ways in which the switches can be arranged to provide this temporary cell storage, but the main schemes fall into three categories, placing buffers at:

- the inputs to the switch
- the outputs of the switch
- the crosspoints of the switching matrix.

These options are shown in Figures 1.6–1.8.

The last option, crosspoint buffering, has a queue at each crosspoint. The disadvantage of this system is that it divides the total buffer space into N^2 different queues rather than N, as with the other two systems.

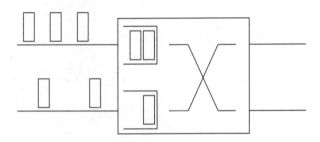

Figure 1.6
Input buffering

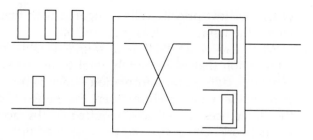

Figure 1.7
Output buffering

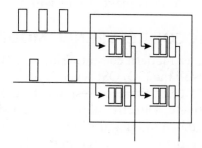

Figure 1.8
Crosspoint buffering

The net effect of this division of resources is an increase in the cell loss probability for the switch, as against the other systems (for the same total amount of buffer space). For the same reason, an output buffer may be shared between a number of outgoing links to benefit from the greater pooling of resources.

The result of much study into these different designs has resulted in the conclusion that output buffering is preferable (especially when this is combined with sharing the available space between all the outputs). In Chapter 5 we will be examining switching from a traffic perspective, and concentrating on output buffering.

1.6   CELL LOSS PRIORITY BIT

There is a part of the cell header that needs to be mentioned here, as it critically affects certain aspects of traffic engineering and design. That is the cell loss priority (CLP) bit, which is used to distinguish between two levels of what is called "space priority". This deals with the conditions under which a cell is allowed to enter a buffer, i.e. its access to buffer "space". A buffer which is deemed full for low priority cells can still allow high priority cells to enter. The effect is to increase the likelihood of loss for low priority cells compared with that for high priority cells. Hence the name "cell loss priority" bit.

What use is it? Well if a source is able to distinguish between information that is absolutely vital to its correct operation (e.g. video synchronisation) and information which is not quite so important (e.g. part of the video picture) then the network can take advantage of the differences in cell loss requirement by accepting more traffic on the network. Otherwise the network loading is restricted by the more stringent cell loss requirement.

So, network nodes may not just be simple first-in first-out finite sized buffers; they can also implement some form of space priority scheme, which ATM cells make use of with the CLP bit in the cell header.

1.7   THE PROTOCOL REFERENCE MODEL

Like other modern communication networks, ATM has a layered structure (recall the ISO/OSI seven layer system). So far, we have mentioned bits and cells; these correspond to the physical layer and ATM layer respectively. Directly 'above' the ATM layer is the ATM Adaptation Layer; the AAL (Figure 1.9). The primary function of the AAL is to organise the data from the higher layers of the terminal into units that will fit within the information field of the ATM cell (48 octets). For example, if a block of computer data is too large for the information field it must be divided into two or more segments (and hence, cells) at the source and reassembled from those segments at the destination. This process, which is illustrated in Figure 1.9, can involve a certain amount of overhead, in the form of header and trailer information for each segment, as well as for the complete block of data.

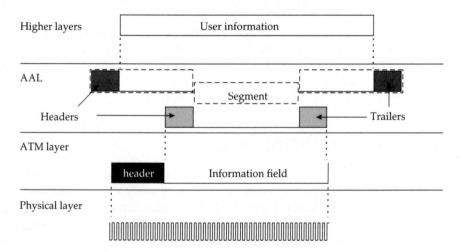

Figure 1.9
The layers of the protocol reference model and the corresponding data units

Precisely how this is done depends on the requirements of the service being transported. A limited set of AAL "types" have been defined in the standards to provide a range of different functions suitable for the currently foreseen service requirements. These are described in detail in [2]. For our purposes, we need to be aware of the fact that the actual user data may not fully fill the 48 octets in the information field. The maximum number is 44, 47 or 48 octets depending on the AAL type being used. This has an impact on the actual cell rate corresponding to a user's information data rate.

1.8 CONTROLLING THE CONNECTIONS

We haven't yet said how connections are established in ATM. We have mentioned that one of the main problems in packet switching is the large variation in delay suffered by packets. ATM also queues cells in nodes across the network, introducing variable delays. How can this be tolerated if an ATM network is supposed to cater for all types of telecommunication — both interactive and non-interactive? Voice services, for example, cannot tolerate large and variable delays, along with rate reduction if the network is congested.

To establish connections (whether virtual paths or virtual channels), ATM operates in a similar way to circuit switching. Upon receiving a connection request, the network has to assess whether or not it can handle the connection, in addition to what has already been accepted on the network. This process is rather more complicated than for circuit switching, because some of the connection requests will be from variable bit-rate (VBR) services. Consequently, the instantaneous bit-rate required by such services will be varying in a random manner over time, as indeed will be the capacity available because some of the existing connections will also be VBR! So if a request arrives for a time varying amount of capacity, and the capacity available is also varying with time, it is no longer a trivial problem to determine whether the connection should be accepted.

In practice such a system will work in the following way: the user declares values for some parameters which describe the traffic behaviour of the requested connection, as well as the loss and delay performance required; the network will then use these traffic and performance values to come to an accept/reject decision and inform the user. If the connection is accepted, the network has to ensure that the connection corresponds to the declared traffic values. This whole process is aimed at *preventing* congestion in the network and ensuring that the performance requirements of each connection are met.

The traffic and performance values agreed by the user and the network form a *traffic contract*. The mechanism which makes the accept/reject decision is called *connection admission control* (CAC), and this resides in the switching nodes in an ATM network. A mechanism is also necessary to ensure subscriber compliance with the traffic contract, i.e. the user should not exceed the peak (or mean, or whatever) cell rate that was agreed for the connection. This mechanism is called *usage parameter control* (UPC) and is situated on entry to the network. If the user does exceed the traffic contract, then the UPC mechanism takes action to protect the network from the effects of this excess, e.g. discarding some of the cells from the non-compliant connection.

CAC and UPC are the two most important traffic control mechanisms in ATM. In order to design algorithms for these mechanisms, we need to understand the characteristics of ATM traffic sources, and the effects these sources have when they are multiplexed through buffers in the network, in terms of the delay and loss suffered by cells. How we design the algorithms is very closely related to how large we make the buffers, and whether any priority mechanisms are proposed. Buffer dimensioning and priority mechanisms depend on how we intend to handle the different services and their performance requirements.

2 Teletraffic Engineering

the economic and service arguments

2.1 SHARING RESOURCES

A simple answer to the question "why have a network?" is "to communicate information between people". A slightly more detailed answer would be: "To communicate information between *all people who would want to exchange information, when they want to*". Teletraffic engineering addresses the problems caused by sharing of network resources among the population of users; it is used to answer questions like: "How much traffic needs to be handled?" "What level of performance should be maintained?" "What type of, and how many, resources are required?" "How should the resources be organised to handle traffic?"

2.2 MESH AND STAR NETWORKS

Consider a very simple example: a telephone network in which a separate path (with a handset on each end) is provided between every pair of users. For N users, this means having $N(N-1)/2$ paths and $N(N-1)$ telephone handsets. A simple cost saving measure would be to replace the $N-1$ handsets per user with just one handset and a 1 to $N-1$ switch (Figure 2.1). A total of N handsets and N switches is required, along with the $N(N-1)/2$ paths. If all N users are communicating over the network at the same time, i.e. there are $N/2$ simultaneous calls (or $(N-1)/2$ if N is odd), then $1/(N-1)$ of the paths and all of the handsets and switches would be in use. So in a network with 120 users, for example, the maximum path utilisation is just under 1%, and handset and switch utilisation are both 100%.

Contrast this with a star network, where each user has a single handset connected to two N to 1 switches, and the poles of the switches are connected by a single path (Figure 2.2). In this example, there are N handsets, $N + 1$ paths, and two switches. However only two users may communicate at any one time, i.e. $3/(N + 1)$ of the paths, $2/N$ of the handsets and both of the switches would be in use. So for a network with 120 users, the maximum values are: path utilisation just under 3%, handset utilisation just under 2% and switch utilisation 100%.

In the course of one day, suppose that each one of the 120 users initiates on average two three-minute calls. Thus the total *traffic volume* is $120 \times 2 \times 3 = 720$ call minutes, i.e. 12 hours of calls. Both star and mesh networks can handle this amount of traffic; the mesh network can carry up to 60 calls simultaneously; the star network carries only one call at a time. The mesh network provides the maximum capability for immediate communication, but at the expense of many paths and switches. The star network provides the minimum capability for communication between any two users at minimum cost, but at the inconvenience of having to wait to use the network.

The capacity of the star network could be increased by installing M switching "units", where each unit comprises two N to 1 switches linked by a single path (Figure 2.3). Thus, with $N/2$ switching units, the star network would have the same communication capability as the mesh network, with the same number of switches and handsets, but requiring

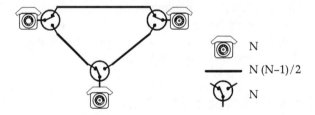

Figure 2.1
The mesh network

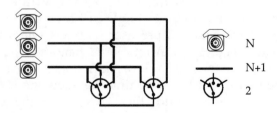

Figure 2.2
The star network

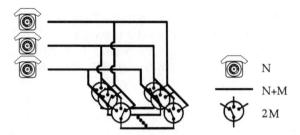

Figure 2.3
The star network with M switching "units"

only $3N/2$ paths. Even in this case, though, the size becomes impractical as N increases, such that reorganisation and further sharing of the switching capacity becomes necessary.

2.3 TRAFFIC INTENSITY

Traffic volume is defined as the *total* call holding time for all calls, i.e. the number of calls multiplied by the mean holding time per call. This is not very helpful in determining the total number of paths or switching units required. We need a measure that gives some indication of the *average workload* we are applying to the network.

Traffic intensity is defined in two ways, depending on whether we are concerned with the workload applied to the network (offered traffic), or the work done by the network (carried traffic). The offered traffic intensity is defined as:

$$A = \frac{ch}{T}$$

where c is number of call attempts in time period T, and h is the mean call holding time (the average call duration). Note that if we let T equal h then the offered traffic intensity is just the number of call attempts during the mean call holding time. The rate of call attempts, also called the call arrival rate, is given by

$$a = \frac{c}{T}$$

So the offered traffic intensity can also be expressed as

$$A = ah$$

For any specific pattern of call attempts, there may be insufficient paths to satisfy all of the call attempts; this is particularly obvious in the case of the star network in Figure 2.2 which has just one path available. A call attempt made when the network is full is blocked (lost) and cannot be carried. If, during time period T, c_c calls are carried and c_l calls are lost, then the total number of call attempts is

$$c = c_c + c_l$$

We then have

$$A = \frac{(c_c + c_l)h}{T} = C + L$$

where C, the carried traffic, is given by

$$C = \frac{c_c h}{T}$$

and L, the lost traffic, is given by

$$L = \frac{c_l h}{T}$$

The blocked calls contributing to the lost traffic intensity obviously do not last for any length of time. The lost traffic intensity, as defined, is thus a theoretical intensity which would exist if there were infinite resources available. Hence the lost traffic cannot be measured, although the *number* of lost calls can. The carried traffic intensity can be measured, and is the average number of paths in use simultaneously (this is intuitive, as we have already stated that it should be a measure of the work being done by the network). As a theoretical concept, however, we shall see that offered, lost and carried traffic prove to be very useful indeed.

Traffic intensity is a dimensionless quantity. It is given the "honorary" dimension of Erlangs in memory of Anders K. Erlang, the founder of traffic theory: one Erlang of traffic is written as 1 E. Let's put some numbers in the formulas. In our previous example we had 240 calls over the period of a day, and an average call duration of three minutes. Suppose 24 calls are unsuccessful, then $c = 240$, $c_c = 216$, and $c_l = 24$. Thus

$$A = \frac{240 \times 3}{24 \times 60} = 0.5 \text{ E}$$

$$L = \frac{24 \times 3}{24 \times 60} = 0.05 \text{ E}$$

$$C = \frac{216 \times 3}{24 \times 60} = 0.45 \text{ E}$$

Later in this chapter we will introduce a formula which relates A and L according to the number of available paths, N.

It is important to keep in mind that one Erlang (1 E) implicitly represents a quantity of bandwidth, e.g. a 64 kbit/s circuit, being used continuously. For circuit switched telephone networks, it is unnecessary to make this explicit: one telephone call occupies one circuit for the duration of one call. However, if we need to handle traffic with many different bandwidth demands, traffic intensity is rather more difficult to define.

One way of taking the service bandwidth into account is to use the MbitE/s (the "megabit-Erlang-per-second") as a measure of traffic intensity. Thus 1 E of 64 kbit/s digital telephony is represented as 0.064 MbitE/s (in each direction of communication). We shall see later, though, that finding a single value for the service bandwidth of variable rate traffic is not an easy matter. Suffice to say that we need to know the call arrival rate and the average call duration, to give the traffic flow in Erlangs, and also the fact that some bandwidth is implicitly associated with the traffic flow for each different type of traffic.

2.4 PERFORMANCE

The two different network structures, mesh and star, illustrate how the same volume of traffic can be handled very differently. With the star network, users may have to wait significantly longer for service (which, in a circuit switched network, can mean repeated attempts by a user to establish a call). A comparison of the waiting time and the delay that users will tolerate (before they give up and become customers of a competing network operator) enables us to assess the adequacy of the network. The waiting time is a measure of performance, as is the "loss" of a customer.

This also shows a general principle about the flow of traffic: introducing delay reduces the flow, and a reduced traffic flow requires fewer resources. The challenge is to find an optimum value of the delay introduced in order to balance the traffic demand, the performance requirements, and the amount (and cost) of network resources. We will see that much of ATM teletraffic engineering is concerned with assessing the traffic flow of cells being carried through the delaying mechanism of the ATM buffer.

2.5 TCP: TRAFFIC, CAPACITY AND PERFORMANCE

So we have identified three elements: the capacity of a network and its constituent parts; the amount of traffic to be carried on the network; and the requirements associated with that traffic, in terms of the performance

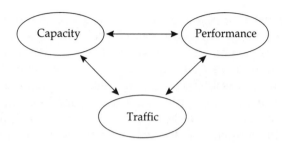

Figure 2.4
Traffic, capacity and performance

offered by the network to users (see Figure 2.4). One of these elements may be fixed in order to determine how the others vary with each other, or two elements may be fixed in order to find a value for the third. For example, the emphasis in dimensioning is on determining the capacity required, given specific traffic demand and performance targets. Performance engineering aims at assessing the feasibility of a particular network design (or, more commonly, an aspect or part of a network) under different traffic conditions; hence the emphasis is on varying the traffic and measuring the performance for a given capacity (network design). Admission control procedures for calls in an ATM network have the capacity and performance requirements fixed, with the aim of assessing how much, and what mix of, traffic can be accepted by the network.

In summary, a network provides the ability to communicate information between users, with the aim of providing an effective service at reasonable cost. It is uneconomic to provide separate paths between every pair of users. There is thus a need to share paths, and provide users with the means to access these paths when required. A network comprises building blocks (switches, terminal equipment, transmission paths), each of which has a finite capacity for transferring information. Whether or not this capacity is adequate depends on the demand from users for transferring information, and the requirements that users place on that transfer. Teletraffic engineering is concerned with the relationships among these three elements of traffic, capacity and performance.

2.6 VARIATION OF TRAFFIC INTENSITY

It is important not to fall into the trap of thinking that a traffic intensity of x Erlangs can always be carried on x circuits. The occurrence of any particular pattern of calls is a matter of chance, and the traffic intensity measures the average, not the variation in, traffic during a particular period. The general principle is that more circuits will be needed on a route than the numerical value of the traffic intensity.

Figure 2.5 shows a typical distribution of the number of call attempts per unit time. If we let this "unit time" be equal to the average call duration, then the average number of "call attempts per unit time" is numerically equal to the offered traffic intensity. In the case shown it is 2.5 E.

This distribution describes the time varying nature of traffic for a constant average intensity. We could define this average, as before, over the period of one day. But is this sensible? What if 240 calls occur during a day, but 200 of the 240 calls occur between 10 am and 11 am? Then the offered traffic intensity for this hour is

$$A = \frac{200 \times 3}{60} = 10 \text{ E}$$

This is significantly larger than the daily average, which we calculated earlier to be 0.5 E. The larger figure for offered traffic gives a better indication of the number of circuits needed. This is because traffic intensity, in practice, varies from a low level during the night to one or more peaks during the day, and a network operator must provide enough circuits to ensure that the performance requirements are met when the traffic is at its peak during the busiest period of the day. The busy hour is defined as a period when the intensity is at a maximum over an uninterrupted period of 60 minutes. Note that the busy hour traffic is still an average: it is an average over the timescale of the busy hour (recall that this is then the maximum over the timescale of a day).

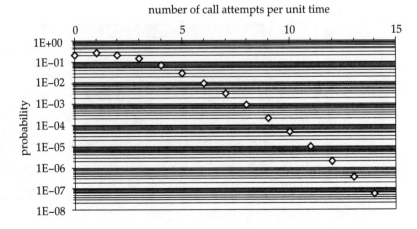

Figure 2.5
The distribution of demand for an offered traffic intensity of 2.5 E

2.7   ERLANG'S LOST CALL FORMULA

In 1917, Erlang published a teletraffic dimensioning method for circuit-switched networks. He developed a formula which expressed the probability of a call being blocked, B, as a function of the applied (offered) traffic intensity, A, and the number of circuits available, N:

$$B = \frac{A^N}{N!} \bigg/ \left(1 + \frac{A^1}{1!} + \frac{A^2}{2!} + \ldots + \frac{A^N}{N!}\right)$$

B is also the proportion of offered traffic that is lost. Hence

$$B = \frac{L}{A}$$

where L is the lost traffic, as before.

The most important assumption made concerns the pattern of arrivals — calls occur "individually and collectively at random". This means they are as likely to occur at one time as at any other time. This type of arrival process is called Poisson traffic. The Poisson distribution gives the probability that a certain number of calls arrive during a particular time interval. We will look at this distribution in more detail in Chapter 4. First, let us plot B against N when $A = 2.5$ E. This is shown in Figure 2.6.

We can read from the graph that the blocking probability is $B = 0.01$ when the number of circuits is $N = 7$. Thus we can use this graph for dimensioning: choose the required probability of blocking and find the

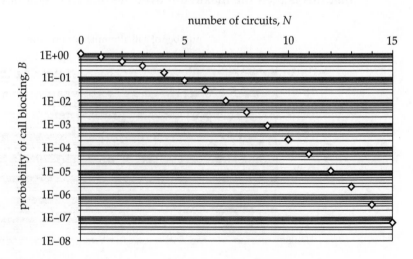

Figure 2.6
The probability of call blocking for A = 2.5 E

number of circuits corresponding to this on the graph. But we don't
want to have to produce graphs for every possible value of offered
traffic.

2.8 TRAFFIC TABLES

The problem is that Erlang's lost call formula gives the call blocking (i.e.
loss) probability, B, given a certain number, N, of trunks being offered
a certain amount, A, of traffic. But the dimensioning question comes
the other way around: with a certain amount, A, of traffic offered, how
many trunks, N, are required to give a blocking probability of B? It is
not possible to express N in terms of B, so traffic tables, like the one in
Table 2.1, have been produced (using iteration), and are widely used, to
simplify this calculation.

The blocking probability specified is used to select the correct column,
and then we track down the column to a row whose value is equal to
or just exceeds the required offered traffic intensity. The value of N for
this row is the minimum number of circuits need to satisfy the required
demand at the specified probability of call blocking.

From the columns of data in the traffic table, it can be seen that, as
the number of circuits increases, the average loading of each circuit
increases, for a fixed call blocking probability. This is plotted in
Figure 2.7 (note that for simplicity we approximate the circuit loading
by the average *offered* traffic per circuit, A/N). So, for example, if we
have 10 circuits arranged into two groups of five, then for a blocking
probability of 0.001 we can load each group with 0.8 E, i.e. a total of
1.6 E. If all 10 circuits are put together into one group, then 3.1 E can

Table 2.1
Table of traffic which may be offered, based on
Erlang's lost call formula

Number of	Probability of blocking, B			
trunks, N	0.02	0.01	0.005	0.001
	Offered traffic, A:			
1	0.02	0.01	0.005	0.001
2	0.22	0.15	0.105	0.046
3	0.60	0.45	0.35	0.19
4	1.1	0.9	0.7	0.44
5	1.7	1.4	1.1	0.8
6	2.3	1.9	1.6	1.1
7	2.9	2.5	2.2	1.6
8	3.6	3.1	2.7	2.1
9	4.3	3.8	3.3	2.6
10	5.1	4.5	4.0	3.1

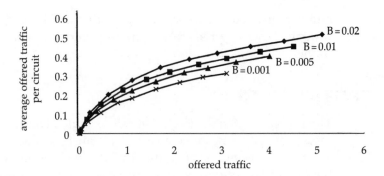

Figure 2.7
Loading efficiency of circuits

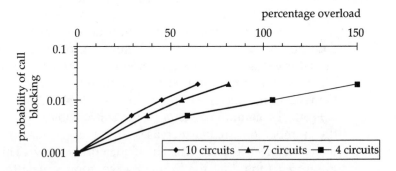

Figure 2.8
Overload capability of circuit groups

be offered for the same probability of blocking of 0.001. In the first case
the offered traffic per circuit is 0.16 E; in the second it is 0.31 E. Thus
the larger the group of circuits, the better the circuit loading efficiency.

However, if we consider how a group of circuits perform under overload, there are disadvantages in having large groups. Here, we use the
rows of data from Table 2.1 and plot, in Figure 2.8, the blocking probability against the percentage increase in offered traffic over the offered
traffic for $B = 0.001$. Small groups of circuits do better under overload
conditions than larger groups; this is because the inefficient small groups
have more "waste" capacity to deal with unexpected overload and the
deterioration in the blocking probability is small. For a large group of
circuits this deterioration can be substantial.

3 Performance Evaluation

how's it going?

3.1 METHODS OF PERFORMANCE EVALUATION

If we are to design a network, we need to know whether the equipment is going to be used to best effect, and to achieve this we will need to be able to evaluate its performance. Methods for performance evaluation fall into two categories: measurement techniques and predictive techniques; with the latter category comprising mathematical analysis and simulation.

Measurement

Measurement methods require real networks to be available for experimentation. The advantage of direct measurement of network performance is that no detail of network operation is excluded: the actual operation of the real network is being monitored and measured. However, there are some constraints. A revenue earning network cannot be exercised to its limits of performance because customers are likely to complain and take their business elsewhere. An experimental network may be limited in the number and type of traffic sources available, thus restricting the range of realistic experimental conditions.

Predictive evaluation: analysis/simulation

In comparing analysis and simulation, the main factors to consider are the accuracy of results, the time to produce results, and the overall cost of using the method (this includes development as well as use).

One advantage of analytical solutions is that they can be used reasonably quickly. However, the need to be able to solve the model restricts the range of system or traffic characteristics that can be included. This can result in right answers to the wrong problem, if the model has to be changed so much from reality to make it tractable. Thus analysis is often used to produce an approximation of a system, with results being produced relatively quickly and cheaply.

Networks of almost arbitrary complexity can be investigated using simulation: systems may be modelled to the required level of precision. Very often, simulation is the only feasible method because of the nature of the problem and because analytical techniques become too difficult to handle. However, simulation can be costly to develop and run, and it is time consuming, particularly when very rare events (such as ATM cell loss) are being measured (although accelerated simulation techniques can reduce the time and cost involved).

3.2 QUEUEING THEORY

Analysis of the queueing process is a fundamental part of performance evaluation, because queues (or waiting lines) form in telecommunications systems whenever customers contend for limited resources. In ATM not only do connections contest, and may be made to queue, but each accepted connection consists of a stream of cells and these also must queue at the switching nodes as they traverse the network.

We will use a queue then as a mathematical expression of the idea of resource contention (Figure 3.1): customers arrive at a queueing system needing a certain amount of service; they wait for service, if it is not immediately available, in a storage area (called a buffer, queue, or waiting line) and having waited a certain length of time, they are served

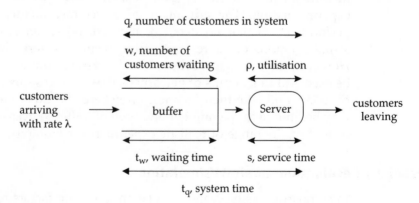

Figure 3.1
The queueing system

and leave the system. Note that the term "customers" is the general expression you will encounter in queueing theory terminology and it is used to mean "anything that queues"; in ATM, customers can be cells, bursts, or connections.

Any queueing system is described by the arrival pattern of customers, the service pattern of customers, the number of service channels, and the system capacity. The arrival pattern of customers is the input to a queueing system and can sometimes be specified just as the average number of arrivals per unit of time (mean arrival rate, λ) or by the average time between arrivals (mean inter-arrival time). The simplest input any queueing system can have is "deterministic", in which the arrival pattern is one customer every t time units, i.e. an arrival rate of $1/t$. So, for a 64 kbit/s constant bit-rate (CBR) service, if all 48 octets of the information field are filled, then the cell rate is 167 cell/s, and the interarrival time is 6 ms. If the arrival pattern is "stochastic" (i.e. it varies in some random fashion over time), then further characterisation is required, e.g. the probability distribution of the time between arrivals. Arrivals may come in batches instead of singly, and the size of these batches may vary. We will look at a selection of arrival patterns in Chapter 4.

The service pattern of customers, as with arrival patterns, can be described as either a rate of serving customers, μ, or as the time required to service a customer, s. There is one important difference: service time or service rate are conditioned on the system not being empty. If it is empty, the service facility is said to be idle. However, when an ATM cell buffer is empty, a continuous stream of empty cell slots is transmitted. Thus the server is synchronised and deterministic; this is illustrated in Figure 1.4.

In the mathematical analysis of an ATM buffer, the synchronisation is often neglected — thus a cell is assumed to enter service immediately upon entry to an empty buffer, instead of waiting until the beginning of the next free slot. For a 155.52 Mbit/s link, the cell slot rate is 366 792 cell/s and the service time per cell is 2.726 µs. However, one in every 27 cell slots is used for operations and maintenance (OAM) cells for various monitoring and measurement duties. Thus the cell slot rate available for traffic is

$$\frac{26}{27} \times 366\,792 = 353\,208 \text{ cell/s}$$

which can be approximated as a service time per cell of 2.831 µs.

The number of service channels refers to the number of servers that can serve customers simultaneously. Multi-channel systems may differ according to the organisation of the queue(s): each server may have its own queue, or there may be only one queue for all the servers. This is of particular interest when analysing different ATM switch designs.

The system capacity consists of the waiting area and the number of service channels, and may be finite or infinite. Obviously, in a real system the capacity must be finite. However, assuming infinite capacity can simplify the analysis and still be of value in describing ATM queueing behaviour.

Notation

Kendall's notation, $A/B/X/Y/Z$, is widely used to describe queueing systems:

$\quad$ A $\quad$ specifies the inter-arrival time distribution
$\quad$ B $\quad$ specifies the service time distribution
$\quad$ X $\quad$ specifies the number of service channels
$\quad$ Y $\quad$ specifies the system capacity, and
$\quad$ Z $\quad$ specifies the queue discipline

An example is the $M/D/1$ queue. Here the M refers to a Memoryless, or Markov, process, i.e. negative exponential inter-arrival times. The D means that the service time is always the same: fixed or "deterministic" (hence the D), and 1 refers to a single server. The Y/Z part of the notation is omitted when the system capacity is infinite and the queue discipline is first come first served. We will introduce abbreviations for other arrival and service processes as we need them.

Elementary relationships

Table 3.1 summarises the notation commonly used for the various elements of a queueing process. This notation is not standardised, so beware ... for example, q may be used, either to mean the average number of customers in the system, or the average number waiting to be served (unless otherwise stated, we will use it to mean the average number in the system).

Table 3.1
Commonly used notation for queueing systems

Notation	Description
λ	mean number of arrivals per unit time
s	mean service time for each customer
ρ	utilisation; fraction of time the server is busy
q	mean number of customers in the system (waiting or being served)
t_q	mean time a customer spends in the system
w	mean number of customers waiting to be served
t_w	mean time a customer spends waiting for service

There are some basic queueing relationships which are true, assuming that the system capacity is *infinite*, but regardless of the arrival or service patterns and the number of channels or the queue discipline. The utilisation, ρ, is equal to the product of the mean arrival rate and the mean service time, i.e.

$$\rho = \lambda s$$

for a single server queue. With one thousand 64 kbit/s CBR sources, the arrival rate is 166 667 cell/s. We have calculated that the service time of a cell is 2.831 µs, so the utilisation, ρ, is 0.472.

The mean number of customers in the queue is related to the average time spent waiting in the queue by a formula called Little's formula (often written as $L = \lambda W$). In our notation this is:

$$w = \lambda t_w$$

So, if the mean waiting time is 50 µs, then the average queue length is 8.333 cells. This relationship also applies to the average number of customers in the system:

$$q = \lambda t_q$$

The mean time in the system is simply equal to the sum of the mean service time and waiting time, i.e.

$$t_q = t_w + s$$

which, in our example, gives a value of 52.831 µs. The mean number of customers in a single server system is given by

$$q = w + \rho$$

which gives a value of 8.805 cells.

The M/M/1 queue

We can continue with the example of N CBR sources feeding an ATM buffer by making two assumptions, but the example will at least give us a context for choosing various parameter values. The first assumption is that the cell arrival pattern from N CBR sources can be approximated by negative exponential inter-arrival times. This is the same as saying that the arrivals are described by a Poisson process. This process just looks at the arrival pattern from a different perspective. Instead of specifying a time duration, the Poisson distribution counts the number of arrivals in a time interval.

The second assumption is that the service times of these cells is described by a negative exponential distribution. In Chapter 6 we will see that the first assumption can be justified for large N. Given the fact that ATM uses fixed length cells (and hence fixed service times), the second assumption is not very accurate! Nonetheless, we can use this example to illustrate some important points about queueing systems.

So, how large should we make the ATM buffer? Remember that the $M/M/1$ queueing system assumes infinite buffer space, but we can get some idea by considering the average number of cells in the system, which is given by

$$q = \frac{\rho}{1 - \rho}$$

In our example, the utilisation resulting from 1000 CBR sources is 0.472, which gives an average system size of 0.894 cells. Subtracting the utilisation from this gives us the average waiting space that is used, 0.422 cells. Not a very helpful result for dimensioning an ATM buffer; we would expect to provide at least some waiting space in excess of one cell. But if we look at a graph (Figure 3.2) of q against ρ, as ρ varies from 0 to 1, then we can draw a very useful conclusion. The key characteristic is the "knee" in the curve around 80%–90% utilisation, which suggests that it is best to operate the system below 80% utilisation to avoid large queues building up.

But we still do not have an idea of how large to make the ATM buffer. The next step is to look at the distribution of system size which

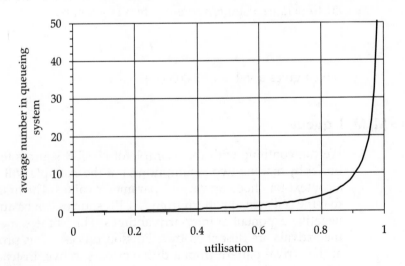

Figure 3.2
Average number of cells in the M/M/1 queueing system

is given by

$$\Pr\{\text{system size} = x\} = (1 - \rho)\rho^x$$

Figure 3.3 shows this distribution for a range of different utilisation values, including the value of 0.472 which is our particular example. In this case we can read from the graph that the probability associated with a system size of 10 cells is 0.0003.

From this we might conclude that a buffer length of ten cells would *not* be adequate to meet the cell loss probability (CLP) requirements of ATM which are often quoted as being 10^{-8} or less. For the system size probability to be less than 10^{-8}, the system size needs to be 24 cells; the actual probability is 7.89×10^{-9}. In making this deduction, we have approximated the CLP by the probability that the buffer has reached a particular level in our infinite buffer model. This assumes that an infinite buffer model is a good model of a finite buffer, and that $\Pr\{\text{system size} = x\}$ is a reasonable approximation to the loss from a finite queue of size x.

Before we leave the $M/M/1$, let's look at another approximation to the CLP. This is the probability that the system size *exceeds* x. This is found by summing the state probabilities up to and including that for x, and then subtracting this sum from 1 (this is a simpler task than summing from $x + 1$ up to infinity). The equation for this turns out to be very simple

$$\Pr\{\text{system size} > x\} = \rho^{x+1}$$

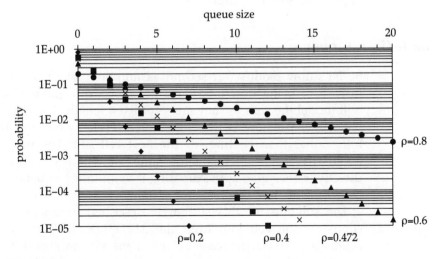

Figure 3.3
System state distribution for the M/M/1 queue

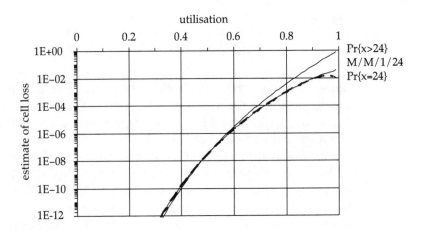

Figure 3.4
Comparison of CLP estimates for finite M/M/1 queueing system

When $x = 24$ and $\rho = 0.472$, this equation gives a value of 7.06×10^{-9} which is very close to the previous estimate.

Now Figure 3.4 compares the results for the two approximations, Pr{system size $= x$} and Pr{system size $\geqslant x$}, with the actual loss probability from the $M/M/1/K$ system, for a system size of 24 cells, with the utilisation varying from 0 to 1. What we find is that all three approaches give very similar results over most utilisation values, diverging only when the utilisation approaches 100%. For the example utilisation value of 0.472, there is in fact very little difference. The main point to note here is that an infinite queue can provide a useful approximation for a finite one.

The M/D/1/K queue

So let's now modify our second assumption, about service times, and instead of being described by a negative exponential distribution we will model the cells as they are — of fixed length. The only assumption we will make now is that they enter service whenever the server is idle, rather than waiting for the next cell slot. The first assumption, about arrival times, remains the same. We will deal with a finite queue directly, rather than approximating it to an infinite queue. This, then, is called the $M/D/1/K$ queueing system.

The solution for this system is described in Chapter 5. Figure 3.5 compares the cell loss from the $M/D/1/K$ with the $M/M/1$ CLP estimator, Pr{system size $= x$}, when the system size is 10. As before, the utilisation ranges from 0 to 1. At the utilisation of interest, 0.472, the difference between the cell loss results is about two orders of magnitude.

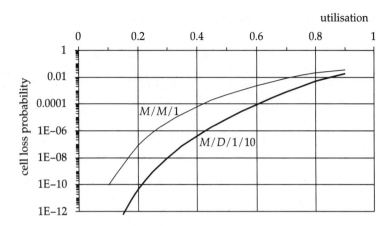

Figure 3.5
Comparison of M/D/1/K and M/M/1 cell loss results

So we need to remember that performance evaluation "answers" can be rather sensitive to the choice of model, and that this means they will always be, to some extent, open to debate. For the cell loss probability in the $M/D/1/K$ to be less than 10^{-8}, the system size needs to be a minimum of 15 cells, and the actual CLP (if it is 15 cells) is 4.34×10^{-9}. So, by using a more accurate model of the system (compared to the $M/M/1$), we can save on designed buffer space, or alternatively, if we use a system size of 24 cells, the utilisation can be increased to 66.8%, rather than 47.2%. This increase corresponds to 415 extra 64 kbit/s simultaneous CBR connections.

It is also worth noting from Figure 3.5 that the cell loss probabilities are very close for high utilisations, i.e. the difference between the two models, with their very different service time assumptions, becomes almost negligible under heavy traffic conditions. In later chapters we present some useful heavy traffic results which can be used for performance evaluation of ATM, where applicable.

Delay in the M/M/1 and M/D/1 queueing systems

ATM features both cell loss and cell delay as key performance measures, and so far we have only considered loss. However, delay is particularly important to real time services, e.g. voice and video. Little's result allows us to calculate the average waiting time from the average number waiting in the queue and the arrival rate. If we apply this analysis to the example of 1000 CBR connections multiplexed together, we obtain the following

$$t_w = \frac{w}{\lambda} = \frac{0.422}{166\,667} = 2.532 \ \mu s$$

The average time in the system is then

$$t_q = t_w + s = 2.532 + 2.831 = 5.363 \text{ μs}$$

Another way of obtaining the same result is to use the waiting time formula for the $M/M/1$ queue. This is

$$t_w = \frac{\rho s}{1 - \rho}$$

For the $M/D/1$ queue, there is a similar waiting time formula

$$t_w = \frac{\rho s}{2(1 - \rho)}$$

In both cases we need to add the service time (cell transmission time) to obtain the overall delay through the system. But the main point to note is that the average waiting time in the $M/D/1$ queue (which works out as 1.265 μs in our example) is *half* that for the $M/M/1$ queue.

Figure 3.6 shows the average waiting time against utilisation for both queue models. The straight line shows the cell service time. Notice how it dominates the delay up to about 60% utilisation. We can take as a useful "rule of thumb" that the average delay arising from queueing across a network will be approximately twice the sum of the service times. This assumes, of course, that the utilisation in any queue will be no more than about 60%. For the total end-to-end delay, we must also add in the propagation times on the transmission links.

So, are these significant values? Well, yes, but taken alone, they are not sufficient. We should remember that they are averages, and cells will

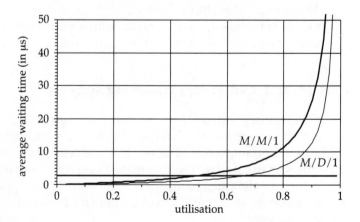

Figure 3.6
Average waiting times for M/M/1 and M/D/1 queues

actually experience delays both larger and smaller. Delay is particularly important when we consider the end-to-end characteristics of connections; all the cells in a connection will have to pass through a series of buffers, each of which will delay them by some "random" amount depending on the number of cells already in the buffer on arrival. This will result in certain cells being delayed more than others, so called "delay jitter", or cell delay variation (CDV).

A pictorial illustration of this is shown in Figure 3.7. Here, we show only the cells of the connection we are monitoring; there is, of course, other traffic which contributes to the queueing in the buffer. The second cell experiences a shorter delay than the first and third cells. This produces a smaller interval between cells 1 and 2, and a longer interval between cells 2 and 3. Variation in delay can be a particular problem for usage parameter control, and we will look at this issue again in Chapter 9.

So much for illustrations, what of concrete examples? If again we use our CBR example (1000 multiplexed CBR 64 kbit/s sources), we can

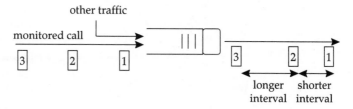

Figure 3.7
Variation in delay for cells passing through a buffer

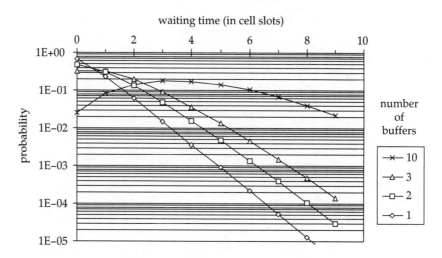

Figure 3.8
End-to-end waiting time distributions

use more of the theory associated with the $M/D/1$ queue to predict the result of passing this stream of cells through a succession of similar queues, and plot the resulting waiting time distribution. The probabilities associated with a cell in the stream being delayed by x time slots having passed through 1, 2, 3 and 10 similar buffers are shown in Figure 3.8. To generate these results, we have assumed that each buffer is independent of all the others, and that they are all loaded at 0.472. The results clearly show the trend for the delay distribution to flatten as the number of buffers increases: as you might expect, the more buffers the cells pass through, the more the probabilities associated with long waits and with short waits tend to equal out.

4 Traffic Models

you've got a source

4.1 LEVELS OF TRAFFIC BEHAVIOUR

So, what kind of traffic behaviour are we interested in for ATM? In Chapter 2 we looked at the flow of calls in a circuit-switched telephony network, and in Chapter 3 we extended this to consider the flow of cells through an ATM buffer. In both cases, the time between "arrivals" (whether calls or cells) was given by a negative exponential distribution: that is to say, arrivals formed a Poisson process. But, although the same source model is used, different types of behaviour are being modelled. In the first case the behaviour concerns the use made of the telephony service by customers — in terms of how often the service is used, and for how long. In the second case, the focus is at the level below the call time scale, i.e. the characteristic behaviour of the service as a flow of cells. Figure 4.1 distinguishes these two different types of behaviour by considering four different timescales of activity:

- calendar: daily, weekly and seasonal variations

- connection: set-up and clear events delimit the connection duration, which is typically in the range 100–1000 seconds

- burst: the behaviour of a transmitting user, characterised as a cell flow rate, over an interval during which that rate is assumed constant. For telephony, the talk-spurt on/off characteristics have durations ranging from a fraction of a second to a few seconds

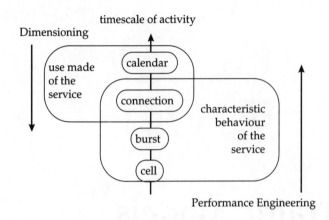

Figure 4.1
Levels of traffic behaviour

- cell: the behaviour of cell generation at the lowest level, concerned with the time interval between cell arrivals (e.g. multiples of 2.831 μs at 155.52 Mbit/s)

This analysis of traffic behaviour helps in distinguishing the primary objectives of dimensioning and performance engineering. Dimensioning focuses on the organisation and provision of sufficient equipment in the network to meet the needs of services used by subscribers (i.e. at the calendar and connection levels); it does require knowledge of the service characteristics, but this is in aggregate form and not necessarily to a great level of detail. Performance engineering, however, focuses on the detail of how the network resources are able to support services (i.e. assessing the limits of performance); this requires consideration of the detail of service characteristics (primarily at the cell and burst levels), as well as information about typical service mixes — how much voice, video and data traffic is being transported on any link (which would be obtained from a study of service use).

4.2   TIMING INFORMATION IN SOURCE MODELS

A source model describes how traffic, whether cells, bursts or connections, emanates from a user. As we have already seen, the same source model can be applied to different timescales of activity, but the Poisson process is not the only one used for ATM. Source models may be classified in a variety of ways: continuous time or discrete time, inter-arrival time or counting process, state based or distribution based, and we will consider some of these in the rest of this chapter. It is worth noting that some models are associated with a particular queue modelling method, an example being fluid flow analysis.

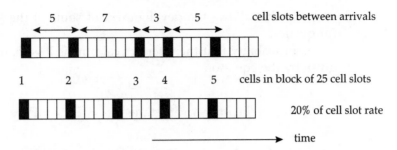

cell slots between arrivals

cells in block of 25 cell slots

20% of cell slot rate

time

Figure 4.2
Timing information for an example cell stream

A distinguishing feature of ATM source models is the way the timing information is presented. Figure 4.2 shows the three different ways in the context of an example cell stream: as the number of cell slots between arrivals (the inter-arrival times are 5, 7, 3, and 5 slots in this example); as a count of the number of arrivals within a specified period (here it is 5 cells in 25 cell slots); and as a cell rate, which in this case is 20% of the cell slot rate.

4.3 TIME BETWEEN ARRIVALS

Inter-arrival times can be specified by either a fixed value, or some arbitrary probability distribution of values, for the time between successive arrivals (whether cells or connections). These values may be in continuous time, taking on any real value, or in discrete time, for example an integer multiple of a discrete time period such as the transmission time of a cell: e.g. 2.831 μs.

A negative-exponential distribution of inter-arrival times is the prime example of a continuous time process because of the "memoryless" property. This name arises from the fact that, if the time is now t_1, the probability of there being k arrivals in the interval $t_1 \rightarrow t_2$ is independent of the interval, δt, since the last arrival (Figure 4.3). It is this

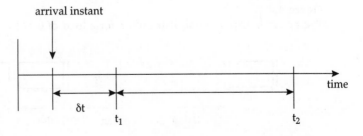

Figure 4.3
The memoryless property of the negative exponential distribution

property that allows the development of some of the simple formulas for queues.

The probability that the inter-arrival time is less than or equal to t is given by the equation

$$\Pr\{\text{inter-arrival time} \leqslant t\} = F(t) = 1 - e^{-\lambda t}$$

where the arrival rate is λ. This distribution, $F(t)$, is shown in Figure 4.4 for a load of 47.2% (i.e. the 1000 CBR source example from Chapter 3). The arrival rate is 166 667 cell/s which corresponds to an average inter-arrival time of 6 μs. The cell slot intervals are also shown every 2.831 μs on the time axis.

The discrete time equivalent is to have a geometrically distributed number of time slots between arrivals (Figure 4.5), where that number is counted from the end of the first cell to the end of the next cell to arrive. Obviously a cell rate of one cell per time slot has an interarrival time of one cell slot, i.e. no empty cell slots between arrivals. The probability that a cell time slot contains a cell, is a constant, which we will call p. Hence a time slot is empty with probability $1 - p$. The probability that

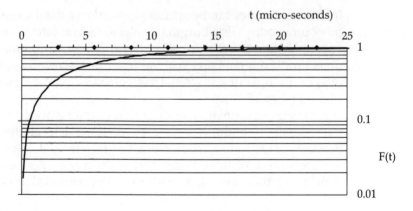

Figure 4.4
The negative exponential distribution for a load of 0.472

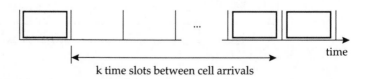

Figure 4.5
Inter-arrival times specified as the number of time slots between arrivals

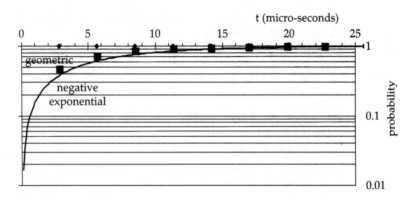

Figure 4.6
A comparison of negative exponential and geometric distributions

there are k time slots between arrivals is given by

$$\Pr\{k \text{ time slots between arrivals}\} = (1-p)^{k-1}p$$

i.e. $k-1$ empty time slots, followed by one full time-slot. This is the geometric distribution, the discrete time equivalent of the negative exponential distribution. The geometric distribution is often introduced in text books in terms of the throwing of dice or coins, hence it is thought of as having $k-1$ "failures" (empty time slots, to us), followed by one "success" (a cell arrival). The mean of the distribution is the inverse of the probability of success, i.e. $1/p$. Note that the geometric distribution also has a "memoryless" property in that the value of p for time slot n remains constant however many arrivals there have been in the previous $n-1$ slots.

Figure 4.6 compares the geometric and negative exponential distributions for a load of 47.2% (i.e. for the geometric distribution, $p = 0.472$, with a time base of 2.831 µs; and for the negative exponential distribution, $\lambda = 166\,667$ cell/s, as before). These are cumulative distributions (like Figure 4.4), and they show the probability that the inter-arrival time is less than or equal to a certain value on the time axis. This time axis is sub-divided into cell slots for ease of comparison. The cumulative geometric distribution begins at time slot $k = 1$ and adds $\Pr\{k \text{ time slots between arrivals}\}$ for each subsequent value of k.

4.4 COUNTING ARRIVALS

An alternative way of presenting timing information about an arrival process is by counting the number of arrivals in a defined time interval. There is an equivalence here with the inter-arrival time approach in continuous time: negative exponential distributed inter-arrival times form a Poisson process:

$$\Pr\{k \text{ arrivals in time } T\} = \frac{(\lambda T)^k}{k!} e^{-\lambda T}$$

where λ is the arrival rate.

In discrete time, geometric inter-arrival times form a Bernoulli process, where the probability of one arrival in a time slot is p and the probability of no arrival in a time slot is $1 - p$. If we consider more than one time slot, then the number of arrivals in N slots is binomially distributed:

$$\Pr\{k \text{ arrivals in } N \text{ time slots}\} = \frac{N!}{(N-k)!k!}(1-p)^{N-k}p^k$$

and p is the average number of arrivals per time slot.

How are these distributions used to model ATM systems? Consider the example of a source that is generating cell arrivals as a Poisson process; the cells are then buffered, and transmitted in the usual way for ATM — as a cell stream in synchronised slots (see Figure 4.7). The Poisson process represents cells arriving from the source to the buffer, at a cell arrival rate of λ cells per time slot. At the buffer output, a cell occupies time slot i with probability p as we have previously defined for the Bernoulli process. Now if λ is the cell arrival rate and p is the output cell rate (both in terms of number of cells per time slot), and if we are not losing any cells in our (infinite) buffer, it must follow that $\lambda = p$.

Note that the output process of an ATM buffer of infinite length, fed by a Poisson source is *not* actually a Bernoulli Process. The reason is that the queue introduces dependence from slot to slot. If there are cells in the buffer, then the probability that no cell is served at the next cell slot is 0, whereas for the Bernoulli process it is $1 - p$. So, although the output cell stream is not a memoryless process, the Bernoulli process

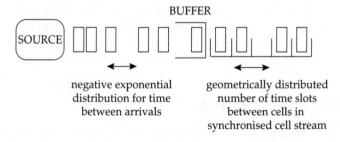

BUFFER

negative exponential distribution for time between arrivals

geometrically distributed number of time slots between cells in synchronised cell stream

Figure 4.7
The Bernoulli output process as an *approximation* to a Poisson arrival stream

is still a useful approximate model, variations of which are frequently encountered in teletraffic engineering for ATM.

The limitation of the negative exponential and geometric inter-arrival processes is that they do not incorporate all of the important characteristics of typical ATM traffic, as will become apparent later.

Certain forms of switch analysis assume "Batch-arrival" processes: here, instead of a single arrival with probability p, we get a group (the batch), and the number in the group can have any distribution. This form of arrival process can also be considered in this category of counting arrivals. For example, at a buffer in an ATM switch, a batch of arrivals up to some maximum, M, arrives from different parts of the switch during a time slot. This can be thought of as counting the same number of arrivals as cells in the batch during that time slot. The Bernoulli process with batch arrivals is characterised by having an independent and identically distributed number of arrivals per discrete time period. This is defined in two parts: the presence of a batch

$$\text{Pr\{there is a batch of arrivals in a time slot\}} = p$$

or the absence of a batch

$$\text{Pr\{there is no batch of arrivals in a time slot\}} = 1 - p$$

and the distribution of the number of cells in a batch:

$$b(k) = \text{Pr\{there are } k \text{ cells in a batch given that there is a batch in the time slot\}}$$

Note that k is greater than 0. This description of the arrival process can be rearranged to give the overall distribution of the number of arrivals per slot, $a(k)$, as follows:

$$a(0) = 1 - p$$

$$a(1) = pb(1)$$

$$a(2) = pb(2)$$

$$\vdots$$

$$a(k) = pb(k)$$

$$\vdots$$

$$a(M) = pb(M)$$

This form of input is used in the switching analysis described in Chapter 5. It is a general form which can be used for both Poisson and binomial input distributions, as well as for arbitrary distributions.

In the case of a Poisson input distribution, the time duration T is one time slot, and if λ is the arrival rate in cells per time slot, then

$$a(k) = \frac{\lambda^k}{k!}e^{-\lambda}$$

For the binomial distribution, we now want the probability that there are k arrivals from M inputs where each input has a probability, p, of producing a cell arrival in any time slot. Thus

$$a(k) = \frac{M!}{(M-k)!k!}(1-p)^{M-k}p^k$$

and the total arrival rate is Mp cells per time slot. Figure 4.8 shows what happens when the total arrival rate is fixed at 0.95 cells per time slot and the number of inputs is 10, 20 and 100 (and so p is 0.095, 0.0475, and 0.0095 respectively). The binomial distribution tends towards the Poisson distribution, and in fact in the limit as $M \rightarrow \infty$ and $p \rightarrow 0$ the distributions are the same.

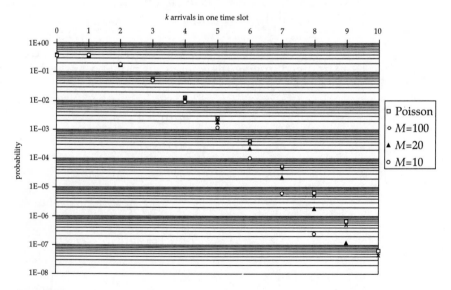

Figure 4.8
A comparison of binomial and Poisson distributions

4.5   RATES OF FLOW

The simplest form of source using a rate description is the periodic arrival stream. We have already met an example of this in 64 kbit/s CBR telephony, which has a cell rate of 167 cell/s in ATM. The next step is to consider an ON-OFF source, where the process switches between a silent state, producing no cells, and a state which produces a particular fixed rate of cells. Sources with durations (in the ON and OFF states) distributed as negative exponentials have been most frequently studied, and have been applied to data traffic, to packet-speech traffic, and as a general model for bursty traffic in an ATM multiplexor.

Figure 4.9 shows a typical teletraffic model for an ON-OFF source. During the time in which the source is on (called the sojourn time in the active state), the source generates cells at a rate of R. After each cell, another cell is generated with probability a, or the source changes to the silent state with probability $1 - a$. Similarly, in the silent state, the source generates another empty time slot with probability s, or moves to the active state with probability $1 - s$. This type of source generates cells in patterns like that shown in Figure 4.10; for this pattern, R is equal to half of the cell slot rate. Note that there are empty slots during the active state; these occur if the cell arrival rate, R, is less than the cell slot rate.

We can view the ON-OFF source in a different way. Instead of showing the cell generation process and empty time slot process explicitly as Bernoulli processes, we can simply describe the active state

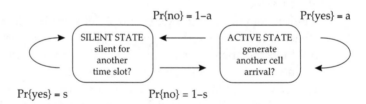

Figure 4.9
An ON-OFF source model

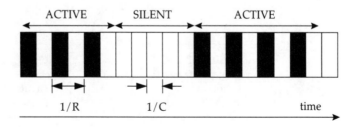

Figure 4.10
Cell pattern for an ON-OFF source model

as having a geometrically distributed number of cell arrivals, and the silent state as having a geometrically distributed number of cell slots. The mean number of cells in an active state, E[on], is equal to the inverse of the probability of exiting the active state, i.e. $1/(1-a)$ cells. The mean number of empty cell slots in a silent state, E[off], is equal to $1/(1-s)$ cell slots. At the end of a sojourn period in a state, the process switches to the other state with probability 1. Figure 4.11 shows this alternative representation of the ON-OFF source model.

It is important to note that the geometric distributions for the active and silent states have different time bases. For the active state the unit of time is $1/R$, i.e. the cell inter-arrival time. Thus the mean duration in the active state is

$$T_{on} = \frac{1}{R} \, E[on]$$

For the silent state, the unit of time is $1/C$, where C is the cell slot rate; thus the mean duration in the silent state is

$$T_{off} = \frac{1}{C} \, E[off]$$

The alternative representation of Figure 4.11 can then be generalised by allowing arbitrary distributions for the number of cells generated in an active period, and also for the number of empty slots generated in a silent period.

Before leaving the ON-OFF source, let's apply it to a practical example: silence suppressed telephony (no cells are transmitted during periods in which the speaker is silent). Typical figures (found by measurement) for the mean ON and OFF periods are 0.96 seconds and 1.69 seconds respectively. Cells are generated from a 64 kbit/s telephony source at a rate of $R = 167$ cell/s and the cell slot rate of a 155.52 Mbit/s link is $C = 353\,208$ cell/s. Thus the mean number of cells produced in an active state is

$$E[on] = R0.96 = 160 \text{ cells}$$

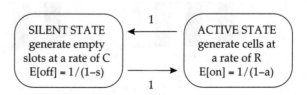

Figure 4.11
An alternative representation of the ON-OFF source model

and the mean number of empty slots in a silent state is

$$E[\text{off}] = C\,1.69 = 596\,921 \text{ cell slots}$$

This gives the model shown in Figure 4.12.

We can also calculate values of parameters a and s for the model in Figure 4.9. We know that

$$E[\text{on}] = \frac{1}{1-a} = 160$$

so

$$a = 1 - \frac{1}{160} = 0.993\,75$$

and

$$E[\text{off}] = \frac{1}{1-s} = 596\,921$$

so

$$s = 1 - \frac{1}{596\,921} = 0.999\,998\,3247$$

The ON-OFF source is just a particular example of a state based model in which the arrival rate in a state is fixed, there are just two states, and the period of time spent in a state (the sojourn time) is negative exponentially, geometrically, or arbitrarily distributed. We can generalise this to incorporate N states, with fixed rates in each state. These multi-state models (called modulated deterministic processes) are useful for modelling a number of ON-OFF sources multiplexed together, or a single, more complex, traffic source such as video.

If we allow the sojourn times to have arbitrary distributions, the resulting process is called a Generally Modulated Deterministic Process (GMDP). If the state durations are exponentially distributed, then the process is called a Markov Modulated Deterministic Process (MMDP). In this case, each state produces a geometrically distributed number of cells during any sojourn period. This is because, having generated

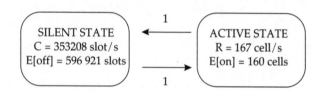

Figure 4.12
ON-OFF source model for silence suppressed telephony

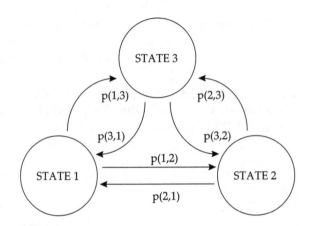

Figure 4.13
The three-state GMDP

arrival i, it generates arrival $i + 1$ with a probability given by the probability that the sojourn time does not end before the time of the next arrival. This probability is a constant if sojourn periods are exponentially distributed because of the "memoryless" property of the negative exponential distribution.

We do not need to restrict the model to having a constant arrival rate in each state: if the arrival process per state is a Poisson process, and the mean of the Poisson distribution is determined by the state the model is in, then we have a Markov Modulated Poisson Process (MMPP), which is useful for representing an aggregate cell arrival process.

For all these state processes, at the end of a sojourn in state i, a transition is made to another state j; this transition is governed by an $N * N$ matrix of transition probabilities, $p(i, j)$ $i \neq j$. Figure 4.13 illustrates a multi-state model, with three states, and with the transition probabilities from state i to state j shown as $p(i, j)$.

5 Switching

up against the buffers

5.1 THE QUEUEING BEHAVIOUR OF ATM CELLS IN OUTPUT BUFFERS

In Chapter 2, we saw how teletraffic engineering results have been used to dimension circuit switched telecommunications networks. ATM is a connection orientated telecommunications network, and we can (correctly) anticipate being able to use these methods to investigate the connection level behaviour of ATM traffic. However, the major difference between circuit switched networks and ATM is that ATM connections consist of a cell stream, where the time between these cells will usually be variable (at whichever point in the network that you measure them). We now need to consider what may happen to such a cell stream as it travels through an ATM switch (it will, in general, pass through many such switches as it crosses the network).

The purpose of an ATM switch is to route arriving cells to the appropriate output. A variety of techniques have been proposed and developed to do switching, but the most common uses output buffering (see Figure 1.7). We will therefore concentrate our analysis on the behaviour of the output buffers in ATM switches. There are three different types of behaviour in which we are interested: the state probabilities, by which we mean the proportion of time that a queue is in a particular state (being in state k means the queue contains k cells) over a very long period of time (i.e. the *steady state* probabilities); the cell loss probability, by which we mean the proportion of cells lost over a very long period of time; and the cell waiting time probabilities, by which we mean the probabilities associated with a cell being delayed k time slots.

To analyse these different types of behaviour, we need to be aware of the timing of events in the output buffer. In ATM, the cell service is of fixed duration, equal to a single time slot, and synchronised so that a cell enters service at the beginning of a time slot. The cell departs at the end of a time slot, and this is synchronised with the start of service of the next cell (or empty time slot, if there is nothing waiting in the buffer). Cells arrive during time slots, as shown in Figure 5.1. The exact instants of arrival are unimportant, but we will assume that any arrivals in a time slot occur before the departure instant for the cell in service during the time slot. This is called an "arrivals first" buffer management strategy. We will also assume that if a cell arrives during time slot n, the earliest it can be transmitted (served) is during time slot $n + 1$.

For our analysis, we will use a Bernoulli process with batch arrivals, characterised by an independent and identically distributed batch of k arrivals ($k = 0, 1, 2, \ldots$) in each cell slot:

$$a(k) = \Pr\{k \text{ arrivals in a cell slot}\}$$

It is particularly important to note that the state probabilities refer to the state of the queue at moments in time that are usually called the "end of time slot instants". These instants are after the arrivals (if there are any) and after the departure (if there is one); indeed they are usually defined to be at a time Δt after the end of the slot, where $\Delta t \to 0$.

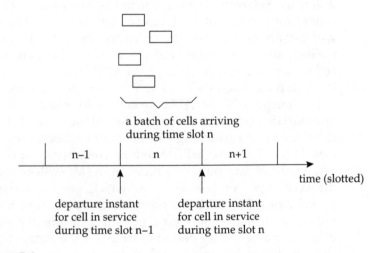

Figure 5.1
Timing of events in the buffer: the arrivals first buffer management strategy

5.2   BALANCE EQUATIONS FOR BUFFERING

The effect of random arrivals on the queue is shown in Figure 5.2. For the buffer to contain i cells *at the end of any time slot* it could have contained any one of $0, 1, \ldots, i+1$ *at the end of the previous slot*. State i can be reached from any of the states 0 up to i by a precise number of arrivals, i down to 1 (with probability $a(i) \ldots a(1)$) as expressed in the figure (note that not all the transitions are shown). To move from $i+1$ to i requires that there are no arrivals, the probability of which is expressed as $a(0)$; this then reflects the completion of service of a cell during the current time slot.

We define the state probability, i.e. the probability of being in state k, as

$$s(k) = \Pr\{\text{there are } k \text{ cells in the queueing system at the end of any time slot}\}$$

and again (as in Chapter 3) we begin by making the simplifying assumption that the queue has infinite capacity. This means we can find the "system empty" probability, $s(0)$ from simple traffic theory. We know from Chapter 2 that

$$L = A - C$$

where L is the lost traffic, A is the offered traffic and C is the carried traffic. But if the queue is infinite, then there is no loss ($L = 0$), so

$$A = C$$

This time, though, we are dealing with a stream of cells, not calls. Thus our offered traffic is numerically equal to λ, the mean arrival rate of

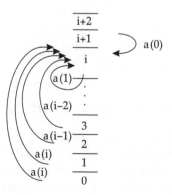

Figure 5.2
How to reach state i at the end of a time slot from states at the end of the previous slot

cells in cell/s, (because the cell service time, s, is one time slot), and the carried traffic is the mean number of cells served per second, i.e. it is the utilisation divided by the service time per cell, so

$$\lambda = \frac{\rho}{s}$$

If we now consider the service time of a cell to be one time slot, for simplicity, then the average number of arrivals per time slot is denoted $E[a]$ (which is the mean of the arrival distribution $a(k)$), and the average number of cells carried per time slot is the utilisation. Thus

$$E[a] = \rho$$

But the utilisation is just the steady state probability that the system is not empty, so

$$E[a] = \rho = 1 - s(0)$$

and therefore

$$s(0) = 1 - E[a]$$

So from just the arrival rate (without any knowledge of the arrival distribution $a(k)$) we are able to determine the probability that the system is empty at the end of any time slot. It is worth noting that, if the applied cell arrival rate is greater than the cell service rate (one cell per time slot) then

$$s(0) < 0$$

which is a very silly answer! Obviously then we need to ensure that cells are not arriving faster (on average) than the system is able to transmit them. If $E[a] \geqslant 1$ cell per time slot, then it is said that the queueing system is *unstable*, and the number of cells in the buffer will simply grow in an unbounded fashion.

5.3 CALCULATING THE STATE PROBABILITY DISTRIBUTION

We can build on this value, $s(0)$, by going back to the idea of adding all the ways in which it is possible to end up in any particular state. Starting with state 0 (the system is empty), this can be reached from a system state of either 1 or 0, as shown in Figure 5.3. This is saying that the system can be in state 0 at the end of slot $n - 1$, with no arrivals in slot n, or it can be in state 1 at the end of slot $n - 1$, with no arrivals in slot n, and at the end of slot n, the system will be in state 0.

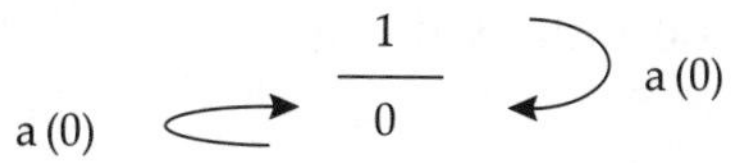

$$\xrightarrow{\quad\quad} \quad \frac{1}{0} \quad \xleftarrow{\quad a(0)}$$

$$a(0) \xleftarrow{\quad\quad}$$

Figure 5.3
How to reach state 0 at the end of a time slot

We can write an equation to express this relationship:

$$s(0) = s(0)a(0) + s(1)a(0)$$

You may ask how it can be that $s(k)$ applies as the state probabilities for the end of time slot $n - 1$ and time slot n. Well the answer lies in the fact that these are steady state (sometimes called "long run") probabilities, and, on the assumption that the buffer has been active for a very long period, the probability distribution for the queue at the end of time slot $n - 1$ is the same as the probability distribution for the end of time slot n. Our equation can be re-arranged to give a formula for $s(1)$:

$$s(1) = s(0)\frac{1 - a(0)}{a(0)}$$

In a similar way, we can find a formula for $s(2)$ by writing a balance equation for $s(1)$:

$$s(1) = s(0)a(1) + s(1)a(1) + s(2)a(0)$$

Again, this is expressing the probability of having 1 in the queueing system at the end of slot n, in terms of having 0, 1 or 2 in the system at the end of slot $n - 1$, along with the appropriate number of arrivals (Figure 5.4). Remember, though, that any arrivals during the current time slot cannot be served during this slot.

Rearranging the equation gives:

$$s(2) = \frac{s(1) - s(0)a(1) - s(1)a(1)}{a(0)}$$

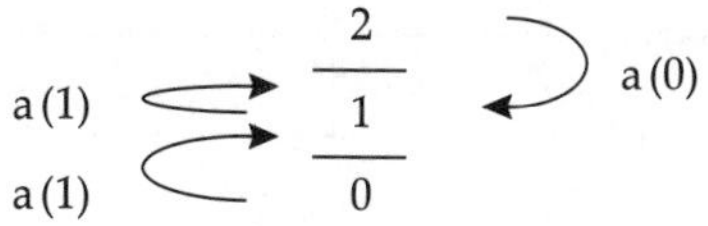

$$\xrightarrow{\quad\quad} \quad \frac{2}{1} \quad \xleftarrow{\quad a(0)}$$

$$a(1) \xleftarrow{\quad\quad}$$

$$a(1) \xleftarrow{\quad\quad} \quad 0$$

Figure 5.4
How to reach state one at the end of a time slot

We can continue with this process to find a similar expression for the general state, k.

$$s(k-1) = s(0)a(k-1) + s(1)a(k-1) + s(2)a(k-2) + \cdots + \\ s(k-1)a(1) + s(k)a(0)$$

which, when rearranged, gives:

$$s(k) = \frac{s(k-1) - s(0)a(k-1) - \sum_{i=1}^{k-1} s(i)a(k-i)}{a(0)}$$

Because we have used the simplifying assumption that the queue length is infinite, we can, theoretically, make k as large as we like. In practice, how large we can make it will depend upon the value of $s(k)$ that results from this calculation, and the program used to implement this algorithm (depending on the relative precision of the real number representation being used).

Now what about results? What does this state distribution look like? Well in part this will depend on the actual input distribution, the values of $a(k)$, so we can start by obtaining results for the two input distributions discussed in Chapter 4: the Binomial and the Poisson. Specifically, let us assume an output buffered switch, and plot the state probabilities for an infinite queue at one of the output buffers; the arrival rate per input is 0.1 (i.e. the probability that an input port contains a cell destined for the output buffer in question is 0.1 for any time slot) and $M = 8$ input and output ports. Thus we have a Binomial distribution

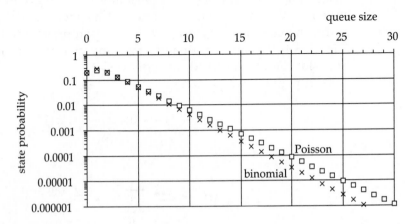

Figure 5.5
State probability distributions for an infinite queue with binomial and Poisson input

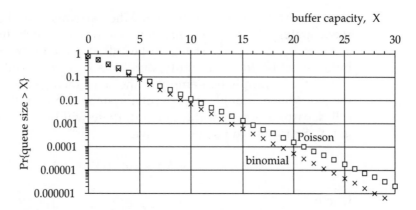

Figure 5.6
Approximation to the cell loss by the probability that the queue state exceeds X

with parameters $M = 8$, $p = 0.1$, compared to a Poisson distribution with mean arrival rate of $Mp = 0.8$ cells per time slot. Both are shown in Figure 5.5.

What then of cell loss? Well with an infinite queue we will not actually have any; in the next section we will deal exactly with the cell loss probability (CLP) from a finite queue of capacity X. Before we do, it is worth considering approximations for the CLP found from the infinite buffer case. As with Chapter 3, we can use the probability that there are more than X cells in the infinite buffer as an approximation for the CLP. In Figure 5.6 we plot this value, for both the Binomial and Poisson cases considered previously, over a range of buffer length values.

5.4 EXACT ANALYSIS FOR FINITE OUTPUT BUFFERS

Having considered infinite buffers, we now want to quantify exactly the effect of a finite buffer, such as we would actually find acting as the output buffer in a switch. We want to know how the CLP at this queue varies with the buffer capacity, X, and to do this, we need to use the balance equation technique. However, this time we cannot find $s(0)$ directly, by equating carried traffic and offered traffic, because there will be some lost traffic, and it is this that we need to find!

So initially we use the same approach as for the infinite queue, temporarily ignoring the fact that we do not know $s(0)$:

$$s(1) = s(0)\frac{1 - a(0)}{a(0)}$$

$$s(k) = \frac{s(k-1) - s(0)a(k-1) - \sum_{i=1}^{k-1} s(i)a(k-i)}{a(0)}$$

For the system to become full with the "arrivals first" buffer management strategy, there is actually only one way in which this can happen *at the end of time slot instants*: to be full at the end of time slot i, the buffer must begin slot i empty, and have X or more cells arrive in the slot. If the system is non-empty at the start, then just before the end of the slot (given enough arrivals) the system will be full, but when the cell departure occurs at the slot end, there will be $X - 1$ cells left, and *not* X. So for the full state, we have:

$$s(X) = s(0)A(X)$$

where
$$A(k) = 1 - a(0) - a(1) - \ldots - a(k - 1)$$

So $A(k)$ is the probability that at least k cells arrive in a slot. Now we face the problem that, without the *value* for $s(0)$, we cannot evaluate $s(k)$ for $k > 0$. What we do is to define a new variable, $u(k)$, as follows

$$u(k) = \frac{s(k)}{s(0)}$$

so
$$u(0) = 1$$

Then

$$u(1) = \frac{1 - a(0)}{a(0)}$$

$$u(k) = \frac{u(k - 1) - a(k - 1) - \sum_{i=1}^{k-1} u(i)a(k - i)}{a(0)}$$

$$u(X) = A(X)$$

and all the values of $u(k), 0 \leqslant k \leqslant X$, can be evaluated! Then using the fact that all the state probabilities must sum to 1, i.e.

$$\sum_{i=0}^{X} s(i) = 1$$

we have

$$\sum_{i=0}^{X} \frac{s(i)}{s(0)} = \frac{1}{s(0)} = \sum_{i=0}^{X} u(i)$$

so

$$s(0) = \frac{1}{\displaystyle\sum_{i=0}^{X} u(i)}$$

The other values of $s(k)$, for $k > 0$, can then be found from the definition of $u(k)$:

$$s(k) = s(0)u(k)$$

Now we can apply the basic traffic theory again, using the relationship between offered, carried and lost traffic at the *cell* level, i.e.

$$L = A - C$$

As before, we consider the service time of a cell to be one time slot, for simplicity; then the average number of arrivals per time slot is $E[a]$ and the average number of cells carried per time slot is the utilisation. Thus

$$L = E(a) - \rho = E(a) - (1 - s(0))$$

and the cell loss probability is just the ratio of lost traffic to offered traffic:

$$CLP = \frac{E(a) - (1 - s(0))}{E(a)}$$

Figure 5.7 shows the state probability distribution for an output buffer of capacity 10 cells (which includes the server) being fed from our eight Bernoulli sources each having $p = 0.1$ as before. The total load is 80%. Notice that that the probability of the buffer being full is very low in the Poisson case, and zero in the binomial case. This is because the arrivals

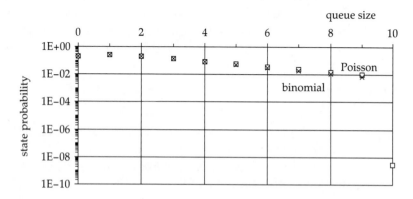

Figure 5.7
State probability distribution for a finite queue of 10 cells and a load of 80%

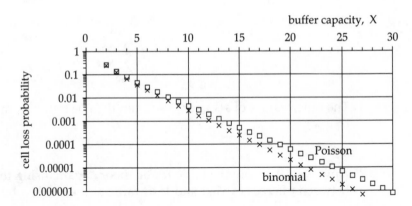

Figure 5.8
Exact cell loss probability against system capacity X for a load of 80%

first strategy needs 10 cells to arrive at an empty queue in order for the
queue to fill up; the maximum batch size with eight Bernoulli sources
is eight cells.

Now we can generate the exact cell loss probabilities for finite buffers.
Figure 5.8 plots the exact CLP value for Binomial and Poisson input to
a finite queue of system capacity X, where X varies from two up to 30
cells. Now compare this with Figure 5.6.

5.5 DELAYS

We looked at waiting times in $M/M/1$ and $M/D/1$ queueing systems in
Chapter 3. Waiting time plus service time gives the system time, which is
the overall delay through the queueing system. So, how do we work out
the probabilities associated with particular delays in the output buffers
of an ATM switch? Notice first that the delay experienced by a cell,
which we will call cell **C**, in a buffer has two components: the delay
due to the "unfinished work" (cells) in the buffer when cell **C** arrives,
U_d, and the delay caused by the other cells in the batch in which **C**
arrives, B_d.

$$T_d = U_d + B_d$$

where T_d is the total delay from the arrival of **C** until the completion of
its transmission (the total system time).

In effect we have already determined U_d, these values are given by
the state probabilities as follows:

$$\Pr\{U_d = 1\} = U_d(1) = s(0) + s(1)$$

Remember that we assumed that each cell will be delayed by at least one time slot, the slot in which it is transmitted. For all $k > 1$ we have the relationship:

$$\Pr\{U_d = k\} = U_d(k) = s(k)$$

The formula for $B_d(k) = \Pr\{B_d = k\}$, accounts for the position of **C** within the batch as well:

$$B_d(k) = \frac{1 - \sum_{i=0}^{k} a(i)}{E[a]}$$

Note that this equation is covered in more depth in Chapter 11.

Now the total delay, $T_d(k)$, consists of all the following possibilities:

$$T_d(k) = \Pr\{U_d = 1 \text{ and } B_d = k - 1\} + \Pr\{U_d = 2 \text{ and } B_d = k - 2\} + \cdots$$

and we account for them all by convolving the two components of delay, using the following formula:

$$T_d(k) = \sum_{j=1}^{k} U_d(j)B_d(k - j)$$

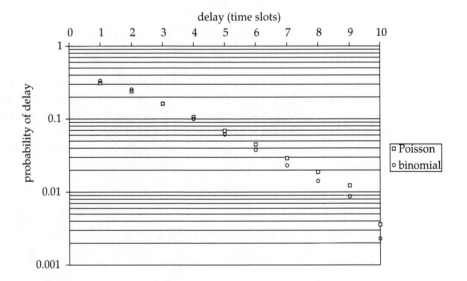

Figure 5.9
Cell delay probabilities for a finite buffer of size 10 cells with a load of 80%

We plot the cell delay probabilities for the example we have been considering (Binomial and Poisson input processes, $p = 0.1$ and $M = 8$, $\rho = 0.8$) in Figure 5.9.

End-to-end delay

To find the cell delay variation through a number of switches, we convolve the cell delay distribution for a single buffer with itself. Let

$$T_{d,n}(k) = \Pr\{\text{total delay through } n \text{ buffers} = k\}$$

Then, for two switches the delay distribution is given by

$$T_{d,2}(k) = \sum_{j=1}^{k} T_{d,1}(j)T_{d,1}(k-j)$$

There is one very important assumption we are making: that the arrivals to each buffer are independent of each other. This is definitely *not* the case if all the traffic through the first buffer goes through the second one. In practice, it is likely that only a small proportion will do so; the bulk of the traffic will be routed elsewhere. This situation is shown in Figure 5.10.

We can extend our calculation for two switches by applying it recursively to find the delay through n buffers:

$$T_{d,n}(k) = \sum_{j=1}^{k} T_{d,n-1}(j)T_{d,1}(k-j)$$

Figure 5.11 shows the end-to-end delay distributions for 1, 2, 3, 5, 7 and 9 buffers, where the buffers have identical but independent binomial arrival distributions, each buffer is finite with a size of 10 cells, and the load offered to each buffer is 80%. Lines are shown as well as markers on the graph to help identify each distribution; obviously, the delay can

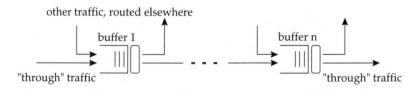

Figure 5.10
Independence assumption for end-to-end delay distribution: "through" traffic is a small proportion of total traffic arriving at each buffer

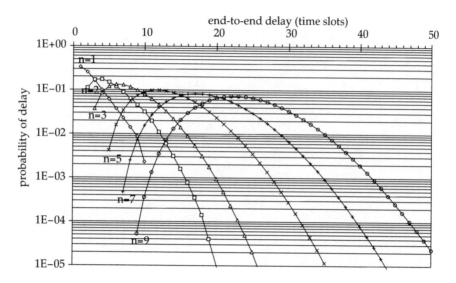

Figure 5.11
End-to-end delay distributions for 1, 2, 3, 5, 7, and 9 buffers, with a load of 80%

only take integer values. As we found in Chapter 3, the delay distribution "flattens" as the number of buffers increases. Note that this is a *delay* distribution, which includes one time slot for the server in each buffer; in Figure 3.8, it is the end-to-end *waiting time* distribution which is shown. So, for example, in the distribution for end-to-end delay through nine buffers, the smallest delay is nine time slots (and the largest delay is 90 time slots, although this is not shown in Figure 5.11).

6 Cell Scale Queueing

dealing with the jitters

6.1 CELL SCALE QUEUEING

In Chapter 3 we considered a situation in which a large collection of CBR voice sources all send their cells to a single buffer. We stated that it was reasonably accurate under certain circumstances (when the number of sources is large enough) to model the total cell arrival process from all the voice sources as a Poisson process.

Now a Poisson process is a single statistical model from which the detailed information about the behaviour of the individual sources has been lost, quite deliberately, in order to achieve simplicity. The process features a random number (a batch) of arrivals per slot (see Figure 6.1) where this batch can vary as $0, 1, 2, \ldots \infty$.

So we could say that in, for example, slot $n + 4$, the process has overloaded the queueing system because two cells have arrived, one more than the buffer can transmit. Again, in slot $n + 5$ the buffer has been overloaded by three cells in the slot. So the process provides short periods during which its instantaneous arrival rate is greater than the cell service rate; indeed if this did not happen, there would be no need for a buffer.

But what does this mean for our N CBR sources? Each source is at a *constant* rate of 167 cell/s, so the cell rate will never individually exceed the service rate of the buffer; and provided $N \times 167 < 353\,208$ cell/s, the total cell rate will not do so either. The maximum number of sources is $353\,208/167 = 2115$ or, put another way, each source produces one cell every 2115 time slots. However, the sources are not necessarily

Number of arrivals in a slot

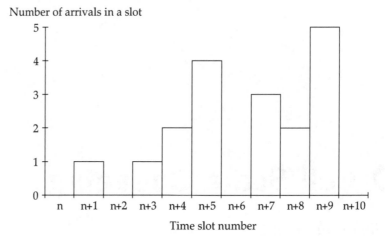

Figure 6.1
A random number of arrivals per time slot

arranged such that a cell from each one arrives in its own time slot; indeed, although the probability is not high, all the sources could be (accidentally) synchronised such that all the cells arrive in the same slot. In fact, for our example of multiplexing 2115 CBR sources, it is possible for any number of cells varying from 0 up to 2115 to arrive in the same slot. The queueing behaviour which arises from this is called cell scale queueing.

6.2   MULTIPLEXING CONSTANT BIT-RATE TRAFFIC

Let us now take a closer look at what happens when we have constant bit rate traffic multiplexed together. Figure 6.2 shows, for a simple situation, how repeating patterns develop in the arrival process, patterns which depend on the relative phases of the sources.

It is clear from this picture that there are going to be circumstances where a simple "classical" queueing system like the $M/D/1$ will not adequately model superposed CBR traffic; in particular, the arrival process is not well modelled by a Poisson process when the number of sources is small. At this point we need a fresh start with a new approach to the analysis.

6.3   ANALYSIS OF AN INFINITE QUEUE WITH MULTIPLEXED CBR INPUT: THE ND/D/1

The $ND/D/1$ queue is a basic model for CBR traffic where the input process comprises N independent periodic sources, each source with the same period D. If we take our collection of 1000 CBR sources, then $N = 1000$, and $D = 2115$ time slots. The queueing analysis caters for

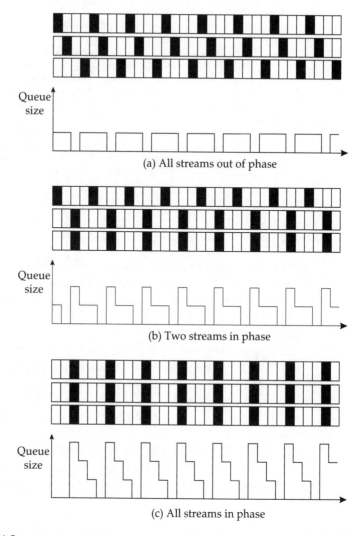

Queue size

(a) All streams out of phase

Queue size

(b) Two streams in phase

Queue size

(c) All streams in phase

Figure 6.2
Repeating patterns in the size of the queue when constant bit-rate traffic is multiplexed

all possible repeating patterns, and their effect on the queue size. The buffer capacity is assumed to be infinite, and the cell loss probability is approximated by the probability that the queue exceeds a certain size x, i.e. $Q(x)$.

$$\text{CLP} \approx Q(x)$$

$$= \sum_{n=x+1}^{N} \left\{ \frac{N!}{n!(N-n)!} \left(\frac{n-x}{D} \right)^n \left[1 - \left(\frac{n-x}{D} \right) \right]^{N-n} \frac{D-N+x}{D-n+x} \right\}$$

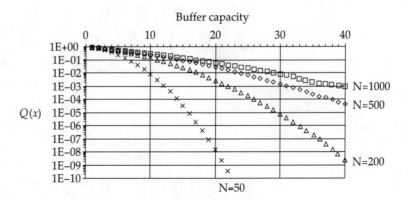

Figure 6.3
Results for the ND/D/1 queue with a load of 95%

Let's put some numbers in, and see how the cell loss varies with different parameters and their values. The distribution of $Q(x)$ for a fixed load of $\rho = N/D = 0.95$ with numbers of sources ranging from 50 up to 1000 is given in Figure 6.3.

Note how the number of inputs (sources) has such a significant impact on the results. Remember that the traffic is periodic, and the utilisation is less than 1, so the maximum number of arrivals in any one period of the constant bit-rate sources (as well as in any one time slot) is limited to one from each source, i.e. N. The value of N limits the maximum size of the queue — if we provide N waiting spaces there would be no loss at all.

The $ND/D/1$ result can be simplified when the applied traffic is close to the service rate; this is called a heavy traffic theorem. But let's first look at a useful heavy traffic result for a queueing system we already know - the $M/D/1$.

6.4 HEAVY TRAFFIC APPROXIMATION FOR THE M/D/1 QUEUE

An approximate analysis of the $M/D/1$ system produces the following equation:

$$Q(x) = \exp\left[-2x\left(\frac{1-\rho}{\rho}\right)\right]$$

Note that

$$\frac{\rho}{2(1-\rho)}$$

is the mean queue length for an $M/D/1$ system, so

$$\frac{2(1-\rho)}{\rho}$$

is the rate at which the queue length decreases. The result actually amounts to approximating the queue length by an exponential distribution: $Q(x)$ is the probability that the queue size exceeds x, and ρ is the utilisation. At first sight, this does not seem to be reasonable; the number in the queue is always an integer, whereas the exponential distribution applies to a continuous variable x; and although x can vary from zero up to infinity, we are using it to represent a finite buffer size. However, it does work: $Q(x)$ is a good approximation for the cell loss probability for a finite buffer of size x.

For this equation to be accurate, the utilisation must be high. Figure 6.4 shows how it compares with our exact analysis from Chapter 5, with Poisson input traffic at different values of load. The approximate results are shown as lines through the origin. It is apparent that, although the cell loss approximation safely overestimates at high utilisation, it can significantly underestimate when the utilisation is low. But in spite of this weakness, the major contribution that this analysis makes is to show that there is a log-linear relationship between cell loss probability and buffer capacity.

Why is this relationship so useful? We can rearrange the equation to specify any one variable in terms of the other two. Recalling the conceptual framework of the Traffic-Capacity-Performance model from Chapter 2, we can see that the traffic is represented by ρ (the utilisation), the capacity is x (the buffer size), and the performance is $Q(x)$ (the approximation to the cell loss probability). Taking natural logarithms of

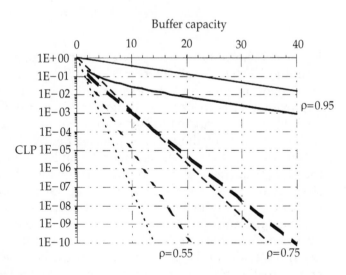

Figure 6.4
Comparing the heavy traffic results for the M/D/1 with exact analysis of the M/D/1/K

both sides of the equation gives

$$\ln(Q(x)) = -2x\frac{(1-\rho)}{\rho}$$

This can be rearranged to give

$$x = -\frac{1}{2}\ln(Q(x))\left(\frac{\rho}{1-\rho}\right)$$

and

$$\rho = \frac{2x}{2x - \ln(Q(x))}$$

We will not investigate how to use these equations just yet. The first relates to buffer dimensioning, and the second to admission control, and both these topics are dealt with in later chapters.

6.5   HEAVY TRAFFIC APPROXIMATION FOR THE ND/D/1 QUEUE

Although the exact solution for the $ND/D/1$ queue is relatively straightforward, the following heavy traffic approximation for the $ND/D/1$ helps to identify explicitly the effect of the parameters:

$$Q(x) = \exp\left[-2x\left(\frac{x}{N} + \frac{1-\rho}{\rho}\right)\right]$$

Figure 6.5 shows how the approximation compares with exact results from the $ND/D/1$ analysis for a load of 95%. The approximate results are shown as lines, and the exact results as markers. In this case the approximation is in very good agreement. Figure 6.6 shows how the approximation compares for three different loads. For low utilisations, the approximate method underestimates the cell loss.

Note that the form of the equation is similar to the approximation for the $M/D/1$ queue, with the addition of a quadratic term in x, the queue size. So, for small values of x, $ND/D/1$ queues behave in a manner similar to $M/D/1$ queues with the same utilisation. But for larger values of x the quadratic term dominates; this reduces the probability of larger queues occurring in the $ND/D/1$, compared to the same size queue in the $M/D/1$ system. Thus we can see how the Poisson process is a useful approximation for N CBR sources, particularly for large N: as $N \to \infty$, the quadratic term disappears and the heavy traffic approximation to the $ND/D/1$ becomes the same as that for the $M/D/1$.

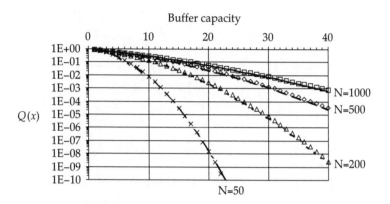

Figure 6.5
Comparison of exact and approximate results for ND/D/1 at a load of 95%

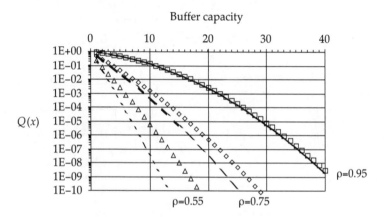

Figure 6.6
Comparison of exact and approximate results for ND/D/1 for a variety of loads,
with N = 200

6.6   CELL SCALE QUEUEING IN SWITCHES

It is important not to assume that cell scale queueing arises only as the
result of source multiplexing. If we now take a look at switching, we
will find that the same effect arises. Consider the simple output buffered
2 × 2 switching element shown in Figure 6.7.

Here we can see a situation analogous to that of multiplexing the CBR
sources. Both the input ports into the switch carry cells coming from any
number of previously multiplexed sources. Figure 6.8 shows a typical
scenario; the cell streams on the input to the switching element are
the output of another buffer, closer to the sources. The same queueing
principle applies at the switch output buffer as at the source multiplexor: the sources may all be CBR, and the individual input ports to

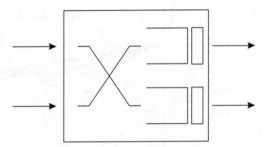

Figure 6.7
An output buffered 2 × 2 switching element

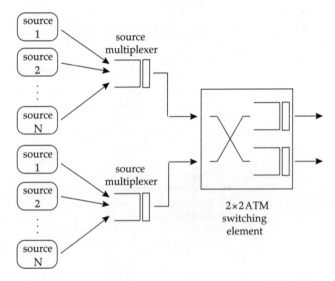

Figure 6.8
Cell scale queueing in switch output buffers

the switch may contain cells such that their aggregate arrival rate is less than the output rate of either of the switch output ports, *but still there can be cell loss in the switch*. Figure 6.9 shows an example of the cell loss probabilities for either of the output buffers in the switch for the scenario illustrated in Figure 6.8. This assumes that the output from each source multiplexor is a Bernoulli process, with parameter $p' = 0.5$, and that the cells are routed in equal proportions to the output buffers of the switching element. Thus the cell scale queueing in each of the output buffers can be modelled with binomial input, where $M = 2$ and $\rho = 0.25$.

So, even if the whole of the ATM network is dedicated to carrying only CBR traffic, there is a need for buffers in the switches to cope with the cell scale queueing behaviour. This is inherent to ATM; it applies even if

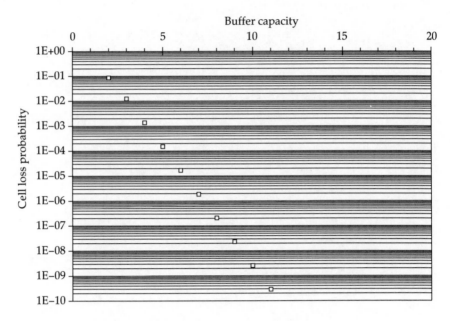

Figure 6.9
Cell loss at the switch output buffer

the network allocates the peak rate to *variable* bit-rate sources. Buffering is required, because multiple streams of cells are multiplexed together. It is worth noting, however, that the cell scale queueing effect (measured by the CLP against the buffer capacity) falls away very rapidly with increasing buffer length — so we only need short buffers to cope with it, and to provide a cell loss performance in accord with traffic requirements. This is not the case with the burst scale queueing behaviour, as we will see in Chapter 7.

7 Burst Scale Queueing

information overload!

7.1 ATM QUEUEING BEHAVIOUR

We have seen in the previous chapter that queueing occurs with CBR traffic when two or more cells arrive during a time slot. If a particular source is CBR, we know that the next cell from it is going to arrive after a fixed duration given by the period, D, of the source, and this gives the ATM buffer some time to recover from multiple arrivals in any time slot when a number of sources are multiplexed together (hence the result that Poisson arrivals are a worst case model for cell scale queueing).

Consider the arrivals from all the CBR sources as a rate of flow of cells. Over the time interval of a single slot, the input rate varies in integer multiples of the cell slot rate (353 208 cell/s) according to the number of arrivals in the slot. But that input rate is very likely to change to a different value at the next cell slot; and the value will often be zero. It makes more sense to define the input rate in terms of the cycle time, D, of the CBR sources, i.e. $353\,208/D$ cell/s. For the buffer to be able to recover from multiple arrivals in a slot, the number of CBR sources N must be less than the inter-arrival time D, so the total input rate $353\,208N/D$ cell/s is less than the cell slot rate.

Cell scale queueing analysis quantifies the effect of having simultaneous arrivals according to the relative phasing of the CBR streams, so we define simultaneity as being within the period of one cell slot.

Let's relax our definition of simultaneity, so that the time duration is a number of cell slots, somewhat larger than one. We will also alter our definition of an arrival from a single source; no longer is it a single cell, but a *burst* of cells during the defined period. Queueing occurs when the total number of cells arriving from simultaneous (or overlapping) bursts exceeds the number of cell slots in that "simultaneous" period.

But how do we define the length of the "simultaneous" period? Well, we don't: we define the source traffic using cell rates, and assume that these rates are on for long enough such that each source contributes rather more than one cell. Originally we considered CBR source traffic, whose behaviour was characterised by a fixed length inactive state followed by the arrival of a single cell. For variable bit-rate (VBR), we redefine this behaviour as a long inactive state followed by an active state producing a "burst" of cells (where burst is defined as a cell arrival rate over a period of time). The state based sources in Chapter 4 are examples of models for VBR traffic.

With these definitions, the condition for queueing is that the *total input rate of simultaneous bursts must exceed the cell slot rate of the ATM buffer.* This is called burst scale queueing. For the N CBR sources there is no burst scale queueing because the total input rate of the simultaneous and continuous bursts of rate $353\,208/D$ cell/s is less than the cell slot rate.

Let's take a specific example, as shown in Figure 7.1. Here we have two VCs with fixed rates of 50% and 25% of the cell slot rate. In the first 12 time slots, the cells of the 25% VC do not coincide with those of the 50% VC and every cell can enter service immediately (for simplicity, we show this as happening in the same slot). In the second set of 12 time slots, the cells of the 25% VC do arrive at the same time as some of those in the 50% VC, and so some cells have to wait before being served. This is cell scale queueing; the number of cells waiting is shown in the graph.

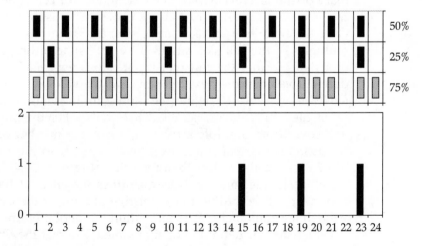

Figure 7.1
Cell scale queueing behaviour

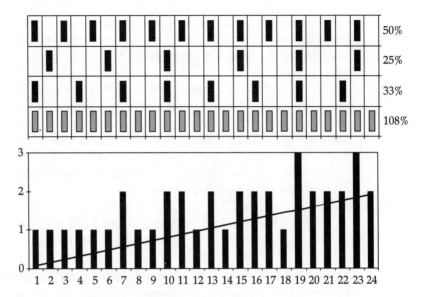

Figure 7.2
Burst scale and cell scale queueing behaviour

Now, let's add in a third VC with a rate of 33% of the cell slot rate (Figure 7.2). The total rate exceeds the queue service rate and over a period of time the number of cells waiting builds up: in this case there are two more arrivals than available service slots over the period shown in the diagram. This longer term queueing is the burst scale queueing and is shown as a solid line in the graph. There is still the short term cell scale queueing, represented by the fluctuations in the number in the queue. ATM queueing comprises both types of behaviour.

7.2 BURST SCALE QUEUEING BEHAVIOUR

The previous example showed that an input rate exceeding the service capacity by 8%, i.e. by 0.08 cells per time slot, would build up over a period of 24 time slots to a queue size of $0.08 \times 24 \approx 2$ cells. During this period (of about 68 μs) there were 26 arriving cells, but only 24 time slots in which to serve them: i.e. an excess of two cells. These two cells are called "excess-rate" cells because they arise from "excess-rate" bursts. Typical bursts can last for durations of milliseconds, rather than microseconds. So, in our example, if the excess rate lasts for 2400 time slots (6.8 ms) then there would be about 200 excess-rate cells that must be held in a buffer, or lost.

We can now distinguish between buffer storage requirements for cell scale queueing (of the order of tens of cells) and for burst scale queueing (of the order of hundreds of cells). Of course, there is only one buffer, through which all the cells must pass: what we are doing is identifying the two components of demand for temporary storage space. Burst scale queueing analyses the demand for the temporary storage of these excess-rate cells.

We can identify two parts to this excess-rate demand, and analyse the parts separately. Firstly, what is the probability that an arriving cell is an excess-rate cell? This is the same as saying that the cell needs burst scale buffer storage. Then, secondly, what is the probability that such a cell is lost, i.e. the probability that a cell is lost, given that it is an excess-rate cell? We can then calculate the overall cell loss probability arising from burst scale queueing as:

$$\Pr\{\text{cell is lost}\} \approx \Pr\{\text{cell is lost} \mid \text{cell needs buffer}\}$$
$$\times \Pr\{\text{cell needs buffer}\}$$

The probability that a cell needs the buffer is called the burst scale loss factor; this is found by considering how the input rate compares with the service rate of the queue. A cell needs to be stored in the buffer if the total input rate exceeds the queue's service rate. If there is no burst scale buffer storage, these cells are lost, and

$$\Pr\{\text{cell is lost}\} \approx \Pr\{\text{cell needs buffer}\}$$

The probability that a cell is lost, given that it needs the buffer, is called the burst scale delay factor; this is the probability that an *excess-rate* cell is lost. If the burst scale buffer size is 0, then this probability is 1, i.e. all excess rate cells are lost. However, if there is some buffer storage, then

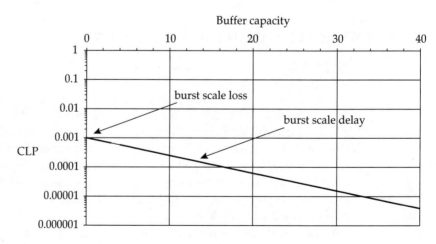

Figure 7.3
The two factors of burst scale queueing behaviour

only some of the excess-rate cells will be lost, (when this buffer storage is full).

Figure 7.3 shows how these two factors combine on a graph of cell loss probability against the buffer capacity. The burst scale delay factor is shown as a straight line with the cell loss decreasing as the buffer capacity increases. The burst scale loss factor is the intersection of the straight line with the zero buffer axis.

7.3 FLUID-FLOW ANALYSIS OF A SINGLE SOURCE

The simplest of all burst scale models is the single ON/OFF source feeding an ATM buffer. When the source is ON, it produces cells at a rate, R, overloading the service capacity, C, and causing burst scale queueing; when OFF, the source sends no cells, and the buffer can recover from this queueing by serving excess-rate cells (Figure 7.4). In this very simple case, there is no cell scale queueing because only one source is present.

There are two main approaches to this analysis. The historical approach is to model the flow of cells into the buffer as though it were a continuous fluid; this ignores the structure of the flow (e.g. bits, octets, or cells). The alternative is the discrete approach, which actually models the individual excess-rate cells.

7.4 CONTINUOUS FLUID-FLOW APPROACH

The source model for this approach was summarised in Chapter 4; the state durations are assumed to be exponentially distributed. A diagram of the system is shown in Figure 7.5. Analysis requires the use of partial differential equations and the derivation is rather too complex in detail

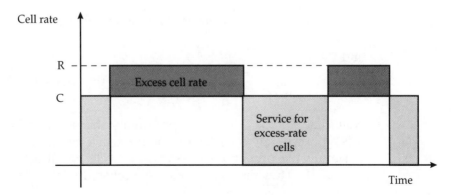

Figure 7.4
Burst scale queueing with a single ON/OFF source

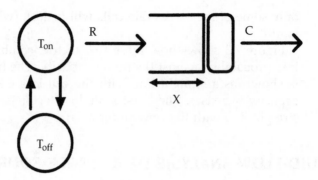

Figure 7.5
Source model and buffer diagram for the continuous fluid-flow analysis

to merit inclusion here. The equation for the excess-rate loss probability is

$$\text{CLP}_{\text{excess-rate}} = \frac{(C - \alpha R)\exp\left(\dfrac{-X(C - \alpha R)}{T_{\text{on}}(1 - \alpha)(R - C)C}\right)}{(1 - \alpha)C - \alpha(R - C)\exp\left(\dfrac{-X(C - \alpha R)}{T_{\text{on}}(1 - \alpha)(R - C)C}\right)}$$

where

$$R = \text{ON rate}$$

$$C = \text{service rate of queue}$$

$$X = \text{buffer capacity of queue}$$

$$T_{\text{on}} = \text{mean duration in ON state}$$

$$T_{\text{off}} = \text{mean duration in OFF state}$$

and

$$\alpha = \frac{T_{\text{on}}}{T_{\text{on}} + T_{\text{off}}} = \text{probability that the source is active}$$

Note that $\text{CLP}_{\text{excess-rate}}$ is the probability that a cell is lost given that it is an excess-rate cell. The probability that a cell is an excess-rate cell is simply the proportion of excess-rate cells to all arriving cells, i.e. $(R - C)/R$. Thus the overall cell loss probability is

$$\text{CLP} = \frac{R - C}{R}\, \text{CLP}_{\text{excess-rate}}$$

We will take an example and put numbers into the formula later on, when we can compare with the results for the discrete approach.

7.5 DISCRETE FLUID-FLOW APPROACH

This form of analysis "sees" each of the excess-rate arrivals. The derivation is simpler than that for the continuous case, and the approach to deriving the balance equations is a useful alternative to that described in Chapter 5. Instead of finding the state probabilities at the end of a time slot, we find the probability that an arriving excess-rate cell finds k cells in the buffer. If an arriving excess-rate cells finds the buffer full, it is lost, and so $CLP_{excess-rate}$ is simply the probability of this event occurring.

We start with the same system model and parameters as for the continuous case, shown in Figure 7.5. The system operation is as follows:

IF the source is in the OFF state AND

a) the buffer is empty, THEN it remains empty
b) the buffer is not empty, THEN it empties at a constant rate C.

IF the source is in the ON state AND
a) the buffer is not full, THEN it fills at a constant rate $R - C$
b) the buffer is full, THEN cells are lost at a constant rate $R - C$.

As was discussed in Chapter 4, in the source's OFF state, no cells are generated, and the OFF period lasts for a geometrically distributed number of time slots. In the ON state, cells are generated at a rate of R. But for this analysis we are only interested in the excess-rate arrivals, so in the ON state we say that excess-rate cells are generated at a rate of $R - C$ and the ON period lasts for a geometrically distributed number of excess-rate arrivals. In each state there is a Bernoulli process: in the OFF state, the probability of being silent for another time slot is s; in the ON state, the probability of generating another excess-rate arrival is a. The model is shown in Figure 7.6.

Once the source has entered the OFF state, it remains there for at least one time slot; after each time slot in the OFF state the source

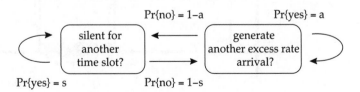

Figure 7.6
The ON/OFF source model for the discrete "fluid-flow" approach

remains in the OFF state with probability s, or enters the ON state with probability $1 - s$. On entry into the ON state, the model generates an excess-rate arrival; after each arrival the source remains in the ON state and generates another arrival with probability a, or enters the OFF state with probability $1 - a$. This process of arrivals and time slots is shown in Figure 7.7.

Now we need to find a and s in terms of the system parameters, R, C, T_{on}, and T_{off}. From the geometric process we know that the mean number of excess-rate cells in an ON period is given by

$$E[on] = \frac{1}{1 - a}$$

But this is simply the mean duration in the ON state multiplied by the excess rate, so

$$E[on] = \frac{1}{1 - a} = T_{on}(R - C)$$

giving

$$a = 1 - \frac{1}{T_{on}(R - C)}$$

In a similar manner, the mean number of empty time slots in the OFF state is

$$E[off] = \frac{1}{1 - s} = T_{off}C$$

giving

$$s = 1 - \frac{1}{T_{off}C}$$

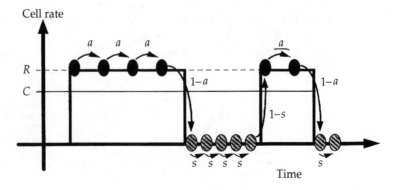

Figure 7.7
The process of arrivals and time slots for the ON/OFF source model

In Chapter 5, we developed balance equations that related the state of the buffer at the end of the current time slot with its state at the end of the previous time slot. This required knowledge of all the possible previous states and how the presence or absence of arrivals could achieve a transition to the current state. For this discrete fluid-flow approach, we use a slightly different form of balance equation, developed according to the so-called "line crossing" method.

Consider the contents of a queue varying over time, as shown in Figure 7.8. If we "draw a line" between states of the queue (in the figure we have drawn one between state (there are 3 in the queue) and state (there are 4 in the queue)) then for every up-crossing through this line, there will also be a down-crossing (otherwise the queue contents would increase forever). Since we know that a probability value can be represented as a proportion, we can equate the proportion of transitions that cause the queue to cross up through the line (probability of crossing up) with the proportion of transitions that cause it to cross down through the line (probability of crossing down). This will work for a line drawn through any adjacent pair of states of the queue.

We define the state probability as

$$p(k) = \Pr\{\text{an arriving excess-rate cell finds } k \text{ cells in the buffer}\}$$

An excess-rate cell which arrives to find X cells in the buffer, where X is the buffer capacity, is lost, so

$$\text{CLP}_{\text{excess-rate}} = p(X)$$

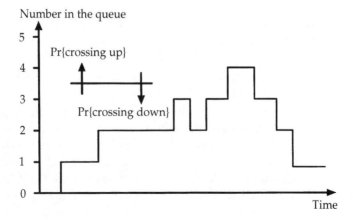

Figure 7.8
The line crossing method

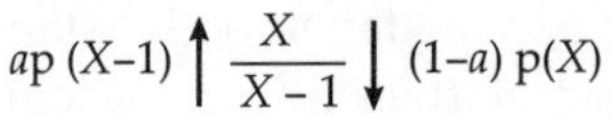

$$ap\,(X{-}1) \uparrow \frac{X}{X-1} \downarrow (1{-}a)\,\mathrm{p}(X)$$

Figure 7.9
Equating up- and down-crossing probabilities between states X and X − 1

The analysis begins by considering the line between states X and $X - 1$. This is shown in Figure 7.9.

Since we are concerned with the state that an arriving excess-rate cell sees, we must consider arrivals one at a time. Thus the state can only ever increase by one. This happens when an arriving excess-rate cell sees $X - 1$ in the queue, taking the queue state up to X, and another excess-rate cell follows immediately (without any intervening empty time slots) to see the queue in state X. So, the probability of going up is

$$\Pr\{\text{going up}\} = a\mathrm{p}(X - 1)$$

To go down, an arriving excess-rate cell sees X in the queue and is lost (because the queue is full), and then there is a gap of at least one empty time slot, so that the next arrival sees fewer than X in the queue. (If there is no gap, then the queue will remain full and the next arrival will see X as well.) So, the probability of going down is

$$\Pr\{\text{going down}\} = (1 - a)\mathrm{p}(X)$$

Equating the probabilities of going up and down, and rearranging gives

$$\mathrm{p}(X - 1) = \frac{1 - a}{a}\mathrm{p}(X)$$

We can do the same for a line between states $X - 1$ and $X - 2$. Equating probabilities gives

$$a\mathrm{p}(X - 2) = (1 - a)s\mathrm{p}(X) + (1 - a)s\mathrm{p}(X - 1)$$

The left-hand side is the probability of going up, and is essentially the same as before. The probability of going down, on the right-hand side of the equation, contains two possibilities. The first term is for an arriving excess-rate cell which sees X in the queue and is lost (because the queue is full), and then there is a gap of at least two empty time slots, so that the next arrival sees fewer than $X - 1$ in the queue. The second term is for an arriving excess-rate cell which sees $X - 1$ in the queue, taking the state of the queue up to X, and then there is a gap of at least two empty time slots, so that the next arrival sees fewer than $X - 1$ in the queue. Rearranging, and substituting for p(X), gives

$$p(X - 2) = \frac{s}{a}p(X - 1)$$

In the general case, for a line between $X - i + 1$ and $X - i$, the probability of going up remains the same as before, i.e. the only way to go up is for an arrival to see $X - i$, and to be followed immediately by another arrival which sees $X - i + 1$. The probability of going down consists of many components, one for each state above $X - i$, but they can be arranged in two groups: the probability of coming down from $X - i + 1$ itself; and the probability of coming down to below $X - i + 1$ from above $X - i + 1$. This latter is just the probability of going down between $X - i + 2$ and $X - i + 1$ multiplied by s, which is the same as going up from $X - i + 1$ multiplied by s. This is illustrated in Figure 7.10.

The general equation then is

$$p(X - i) = \frac{s}{a}p(X - i + 1)$$

The state probabilities form a geometric progression, which can be expressed in terms of p(X), a and s, for $i > 0$:

$$p(X - i) = \left(\frac{s}{a}\right)^i \frac{1 - a}{s}p(X)$$

The probabilities must sum to 1, so

$$\sum_{i=0}^{X} p(X - i) = p(X) + \sum_{i=1}^{X} \left(\frac{s}{a}\right)^i \frac{1 - a}{s}p(X) = 1$$

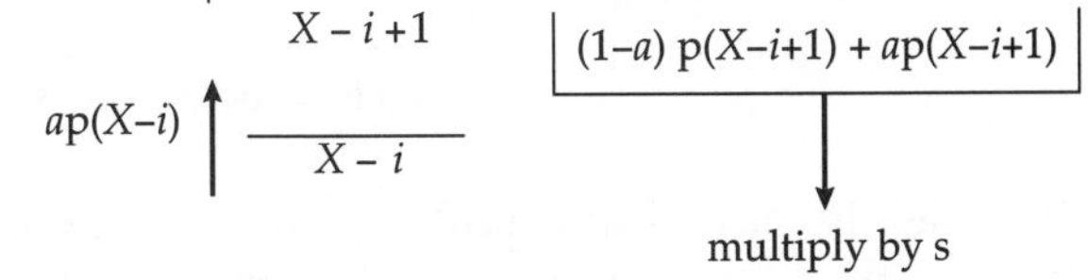

Figure 7.10
Equating up- and down-crossing probabilities in the general case

which can be rearranged to give the probability that an excess-rate arrival sees a full queue, i.e. the excess-rate cell loss probability

$$p(X) = \frac{1}{1 + \sum_{i=1}^{X} \left(\frac{s}{a}\right)^i \frac{1-a}{s}}$$

This can be rewritten as

$$p(X) = \frac{1}{1 + \left(\left(\frac{s}{a}\right)^X - 1\right)\left(\frac{1-a}{s-a}\right)}$$

which is valid except when $a = s$ (in which case the previous formula must be used). As in the case of the continuous fluid-flow analysis, the overall cell loss probability is given by

$$CLP = \frac{R-C}{R} CLP_{excess-rate} = \frac{R-C}{R} p(X)$$

7.6 COMPARING THE DISCRETE AND CONTINUOUS FLUID-FLOW APPROACHES

Let's use the practical example of silence-suppressed telephony, with the following parameter values:

$$R = 167 \text{ cell/s}$$

$$T_{on} = 0.96 \text{ seconds}$$

$$T_{off} = 1.69 \text{ seconds}$$

thus

$$\alpha = \frac{0.96}{0.96 + 1.69} = 0.362$$

and the mean arrival rate

$$\lambda = \alpha R = 60.5 \text{ cell/s}$$

In order to have burst scale queueing, the service capacity, C, must be less than the cell rate in the active state, R. Obviously this does not correspond to a normal ATM buffer operating at 353 208 cell/s. We will see, though, that one application of this analysis is in connection

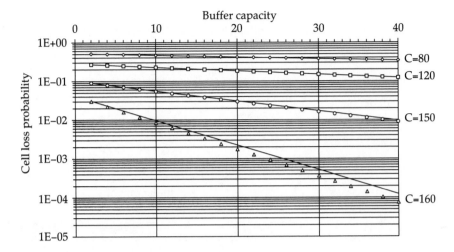

Figure 7.11
Cell loss probability against buffer capacity for a single ON/OFF source

admission control for estimating a bandwidth value, C, to allocate to a source in order to meet a cell loss probability requirement. Figure 7.11 shows the overall cell loss probability plotted against the buffer capacity, X, as the service capacity is varied between the mean and peak cell rates of the source. The discrete fluid-flow results are shown as markers, and the continuous as solid lines.

As the service capacity gets closer to the ON rate, R, the gradient steepens. This means that the buffer is better able to cope with the bursts of excess-rate cells. We can see more clearly why this is so by looking at Table 7.1, which shows the average number of excess-rate cells in an active period. When this number is large relative to the capacity of the buffer, then the buffer does not cope very well because it only takes a fraction of an average burst to fill it up. It would not make much difference if there was no buffer space — there is so little difference to the cell loss over the range of buffer capacity shown. The buffer only makes a difference to the cell loss if the average excess-rate burst length is less than the buffer capacity, i.e. when it would take a number of bursts to fill the buffer. Notice that it is only in these circumstances that the discrete and continuous fluid-flow results show any difference; and then the discrete approach is more accurate because it does not include the "fractions" of cells allowed by the continuous fluid-flow analysis. These small amounts actually represent quite a large proportion of an excess-rate burst when the average number of excess-rate cells in the burst is small.

Figure 7.12 illustrates the strong influence of the average state durations on the results for cell loss probability. Here, $C = 150$ cell/s, with

Table 7.1
Average number of excess-rate cells in an
active period

Capacity (cell/s)	Average number of excess-rate cells per active state
80	83.52
120	45.12
150	16.32
160	6.72

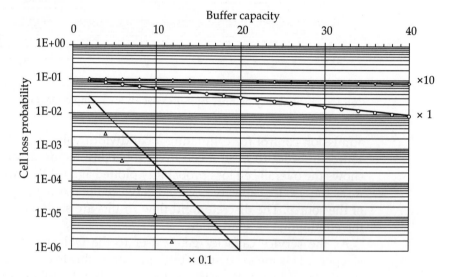

Figure 7.12
The effect of scaling the mean state durations, T_{on} and T_{off}, when C = 150 cell/s

other parameter values as before, and the T_{on} and T_{off} values have been
scaled by 0.1, 1, and 10. In each case the load on the buffer remains
constant at a value of

$$\alpha \frac{R}{C} = 0.362 \frac{167}{150} = 0.403$$

7.7   MULTIPLE ON/OFF SOURCES OF THE SAME TYPE

Let's now consider burst scale queueing when there are multiple
ON/OFF sources being fed through an ATM buffer. Figure 7.13 shows a
diagram of the system, with the relevant source and buffer parameters.
There are N identical sources, each operating independently, sending
cells into an ATM buffer of service capacity C cell/s and finite size X

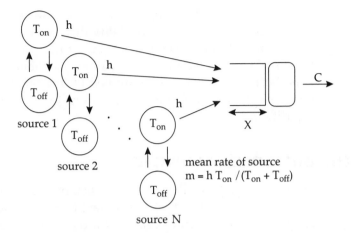

Figure 7.13
Multiple ON/OFF sources feeding an ATM buffer

cells. The average ON and OFF durations are denoted T_{on} and T_{off}, as before; the cell rate in the active state is h cell/s, so the mean cell rate for each source is

$$m = h \frac{T_{on}}{T_{on} + T_{off}}$$

and the probability that the source is active is

$$\alpha = \frac{m}{h} = \frac{T_{on}}{T_{on} + T_{off}}$$

which is also called the "activity factor".

The condition for burst scale queueing is that the total input rate from active sources must be greater than the service rate of the buffer. An important parameter, then, is how many times the peak rate, h, fits into the service capacity, C, denoted by N_0:

$$N_0 = \frac{C}{h}$$

This may well not be an integer value. If we round the value up, to $\lceil N_0 \rceil$ (this notation means take the first integer above N_0), this gives the minimum number of sources required for burst scale queueing to take place. If we round the value down, to $\lfloor N_0 \rfloor$ (this notation means take the first integer below N_0), this gives the maximum number of sources we can have in the system *without* having burst scale queueing.

We saw earlier in the chapter that the burst scale queueing behaviour can be separated into two components: the burst scale loss factor, which is the probability that a cell is an excess-rate cell; and the burst scale delay factor, which is the probability that a cell is lost given that it is an excess-rate cell. Both factors contribute to quantifying the cell loss: the burst scale loss factor gives the cell loss probability, if we assume there is no buffer. This value is multiplied by the burst scale delay factor to give the cell loss probability if we assume there *is* a buffer of some finite capacity.

7.8   THE BUFFERLESS APPROACH

For multiple ON/OFF sources, we start by assuming there is no buffer and calculate the burst scale loss factor. For the single source, this is simply the proportion of cells that are excess-rate cells, i.e. $(R - C)/R$, or with the new parameters, $(h - C)/h$. Another way of looking at this is the *mean* excess rate divided by the *mean* arrival rate:

$$\text{Pr\{cell needs buffer\}} = \frac{\alpha(h - C)}{m} = \frac{\alpha(h - C)}{\alpha h} = \frac{h - C}{h}$$

The probability of an excess rate of $h - C$ is the same as the probability that the source is active, i.e. α, hence the mean excess rate is just $\alpha(h - C)$. In the case of multiple sources, we need to calculate the probability that n sources are active, where $N_0 < n \leqslant N$ and multiply by the excess rate, $nh - C$. This probability is given by the binomial distribution

$$p_n = \frac{N!}{n!(N - n)!} \alpha^n (1 - \alpha)^{N-n}$$

and so the mean excess rate is

$$\sum_{n=\lceil N_0 \rceil}^{N} p_n(nh - C)$$

The mean arrival rate is simply Nm, so the probability that a cell needs the buffer is given by the ratio of the mean excess rate to the mean arrival rate:

$$\text{Pr\{cell needs buffer\}} = \frac{\displaystyle\sum_{n=\lceil N_0 \rceil}^{N} p_n(nh - C)}{Nm}$$

which, if we substitute for $C = N_0 h$ and $\alpha = m/h$, gives

$$\text{Pr\{cell needs buffer\}} = \frac{\displaystyle\sum_{n=\lceil N_0\rceil}^{N} p_n(n - N_0)}{N\alpha}$$

Let's put some numbers into this formula, using the example of two different types of video source, each with a mean bit-rate of 768 kbit/s and peak bit-rates of either 4.608 Mbit/s or 9.216 Mbit/s. The corresponding cell rates are $m = 2000$ cell/s and $h = 12000$ cell/s or 24000 cell/s, and the other parameter values are shown in Table 7.2.

Figure 7.14 shows how the probability that a cell needs the buffer, increases with the number of video sources being multiplexed through the buffer. The minimum number of sources needed to produce burst scale queueing is 30 (for $h = 12\,000$) or 15 (for $h = 24\,000$). The results show that about twice these values (60, and 30, respectively) produce "loss" probabilities of about 10^{-10}, increasing to between 10^{-1} and 10^{-2} for 150 of either source (see Figure 7.14). For both types of source the mean rate, m, is 2000 cell/s, so the average load offered to the buffer, as a fraction of its service capacity, ranges from $30 \times 2000/353\,208 \approx 17\%$ up to $150 \times 2000/353\,208 \approx 85\%$.

We know from Chapter 4 that the binomial distribution can be approximated by the Poisson distribution when the number of sources, N, becomes large. This can be used to provide an approximate result for Pr{cell needs buffer}, the burst scale loss factor, and it has the advantage of being less demanding computationally because there is no summation.

$$\text{Pr\{cell needs buffer\}} \approx \frac{1}{(1-\rho)^2 N_0} \frac{(\rho N_0)^{\lfloor N_0\rfloor}}{\lfloor N_0\rfloor!} e^{-\rho N_0}$$

where the offered load, ρ, is given by

$$\rho = \frac{Nm}{C} = N\frac{m}{h}\frac{h}{C} = \frac{N\alpha}{N_0}$$

Table 7.2
Parameter values

h(cell/s)	$\alpha = \dfrac{2000}{h}$	$N_0 = \dfrac{353\,207.55}{h}$
12 000	0.167	29.43
24 000	0.083	14.72

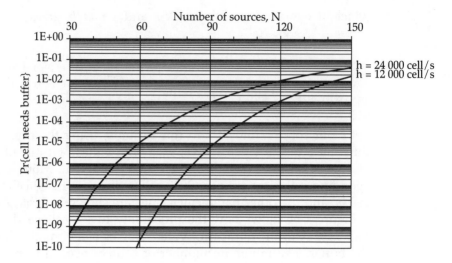

Figure 7.14
The bufferless approach — results for multiple ON/OFF sources

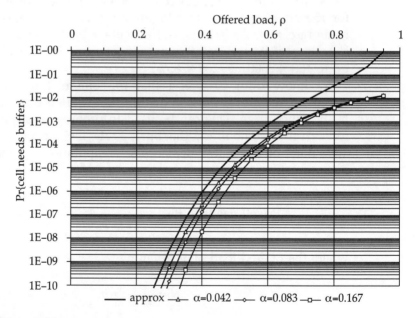

Figure 7.15
An approximation to the burst scale loss factor

Figure 7.15 shows results for ON/OFF sources with peak rate $h = 12\,000$ cell/s, and mean rates varying from $m = 2000$ cell/s ($\alpha = 0.167$) down to 500 cell/s ($\alpha = 0.042$). N_0 is fixed at 29.43, and the graph plots the "loss" probability varying with the offered load, ρ. We can see that for any particular value of ρ the burst scale loss factor increases, as the activity factor, α, decreases, towards an upper limit given by the approximate result. The approximation thus gives a conservative estimate of the probability that a cell needs the buffer. Note that as the activity factor decreases, the number of sources must increase to maintain the constant load, taking it into the region for which the Poisson approximation is valid.

How does this Poisson approximation change our view of the source process? Instead of considering N identical ON/OFF sources each with probability, α, of being in the active state and producing a burst of fixed rate h, we are modelling the traffic as just one Poisson source which produces overlapping bursts. The approximation equates the average number of active sources with the average number of bursts in progress. It's similar to our definition of traffic intensity, but at the burst level.

The average number of active sources is simply $N\alpha$; now, recalling that the probability of being active is related to the average durations in the ON and OFF states:

$$\alpha = \frac{T_{on}}{T_{on} + T_{off}}$$

we can substitute for α to obtain

$$\text{average number of active sources} = T_{on}\frac{N}{T_{on} + T_{off}} = T_{on}\lambda$$

which is the average burst duration multiplied by the burst rate, λ (each source produces one burst every cycle time, $T_{on} + T_{off}$). This is the average number of bursts in progress.

7.9   THE BURST SCALE DELAY MODEL

We are now in a position to extend the burst scale analysis to finding the probability that an excess-rate cell is lost given that it is an excess-rate cell. With the bufferless approach, this probability is 1; every excess-rate cell is lost because we assume there is no buffer in which to store it temporarily. Now we assume that there is a finite amount of buffer space, X, as shown in Figure 7.13.

We will view the N ON/OFF sources as a single Poisson source producing bursts of cell rate h and duration T_{on} at a rate of λ bursts per second, where

$$\lambda = \frac{N}{T_{on} + T_{off}}$$

Note that there is now no limit to the number of overlapping bursts; the Poisson model can exceed N simultaneous bursts. But if N is sufficiently large, the approximation to a Poisson source is reasonable. The average number of cells per burst, b, is given by:

$$b = T_{on}h$$

so the load offered to the queue, as a fraction of the service capacity is

$$\rho = \frac{b\lambda}{C}$$

If we substitute for b and λ (just to check) we obtain

$$\rho = \frac{T_{on}h\dfrac{N}{T_{on} + T_{off}}}{C} = \frac{Nm}{C}$$

which is what we had for the bufferless model.

An approximate analysis of this burst scale delay model uses the $M/M/N$ queueing system (where the number of parallel servers, N, is taken to be the maximum number of bursts which can fit into the service capacity of the ATM buffer, N_0) to give the following estimate for the probability of loss:

$$CLP_{excess-rate} = \exp\left[-N_0\frac{X}{b}\frac{(1-\rho)^3}{4\rho + 1}\right]$$

This is similar in form to the heavy traffic approximations of Chapter 6; an exponential function of buffer capacity and utilisation. Note that the buffer capacity here can be considered in units of the average burst length, i.e. as X/b.

Recall that for the $ND/D/1$ approximation, N, the number of CBR sources, is in the denominator of the exponential function. With a constant load, as N increases, the gradient on the graph of cell loss against buffer capacity decreases, i.e. the buffer is less able to cope with more sources of smaller fixed cell rate. In contrast, this burst scale delay result has N_0 in the numerator of the exponential function. N_0 is the minimum number of overlapping bursts required for burst scale queueing. As N_0 increases, so does the gradient, and the buffer is better able to cope with more sources of smaller ON rates. Why? If it takes more bursts to achieve queueing in the buffer then the period of overlap will be smaller, reducing the effective size of the excess-rate burst. An intuitive way of viewing this is to *think* of b/N_0 as the average excess-rate burst length; then N_0X/b can be considered as the buffer capacity in units of the average excess-rate burst length.

Let's continue with the example of the video sources we used earlier. The mean cell rate for both types of source is $m = 2000$ cell/s and the peak cell rates are either $h = 12\,000$ cell/s or $24\,000$ cell/s. What we still need to specify, are the state durations. If we assume that the ON state is equivalent to a highly active video frame, then we can use a value of 40 ms for T_{on}, which means the average number of cells per burst is $0.04 \times 12\,000 = 480$ cells or 960 cells respectively. T_{off} is given by

$$T_{off} = T_{on}\frac{h - m}{m}$$

so T_{off} takes values of 0.2 seconds or 0.44 seconds respectively. The ON/OFF source cycle times $(T_{on} + T_{off})$ are 0.24 s and 0.48 s, so the burst rates for the equivalent Poisson source of bursts are 4.167 (i.e. 1/0.24) or 2.083 times the number of sources, N, respectively.

Figure 7.16 shows the effect of the buffer capacity on the excess-rate cell loss when there are 60 sources, giving an offered load of 0.34. The results for three types of source are shown: the two just described, and then the higher peak rate source with an average active state duration of half the original. This makes the average burst length, b, the same as that for the lower rate source. We can then make a fair assessment of the impact of N_0, with b and ρ kept constant. It is clear then that as the peak rate decreases, and therefore N_0 increases, the buffer is better able to cope with the excess-rate bursts.

Figure 7.17 shows how the two factors which make up the overall cell loss probability are combined. The buffer capacity value was set

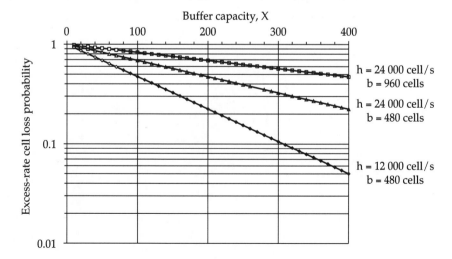

Figure 7.16
Probability of excess-rate cell loss

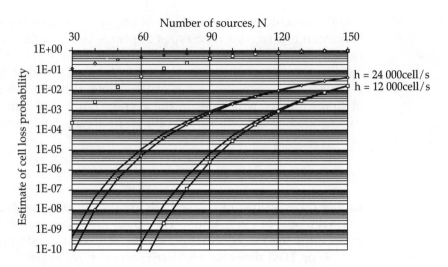

Figure 7.17
Combining results for burst scale delay factor with the burst scale loss factor

at 400 cells. This corresponds to a maximum waiting time of 1.1 ms. The burst scale delay factor is shown for the two different peak rates as the curves with markers only. These results tend to an excess-rate loss probability of 1 as the number of sources, and hence the offered load increases. The burst scale loss results from Figure 7.14 are shown as the lines without markers. The overall cell loss probabilities are the product of the two factors and are the results shown with both lines and markers. Notice that the extra benefit gained by having a large buffer for burst scale queueing, does not appear to be that significant, for the situation considered here.

8 Connection Admission Control

the net that likes to say YES!

No network operator likes to turn away business; if it does so too often customers are likely to take their business elsewhere. Yet if the operator always accepts any connection request, the network may become congested, unable to meet the negotiated performance objectives for the connections already established, with the likely outcome that many customers *will* take their business elsewhere.

Connection admission control (CAC) is the name for that mechanism which has to decide whether or not the bandwidth and performance requirements of a new connection can be supported by the network, in addition to those of the connections already established. If the new connection is accepted, then the bandwidth and performance requirements form a traffic contract between the user and the network. We have seen in Chapter 7, the impact that changes in traffic parameter values have on performance, whether it is the duration of a peak rate burst, or the actual cell rate of a state. It is important then for the network to be able to ensure that the traffic does not exceed its negotiated parameter values. This is the function of usage parameter control. This in turn ensures that the network meets the performance requirements for all the connections it has admitted. Together, connection admission control and usage parameter control (UPC) are the main components in a traffic control framework which aims to prevent congestion occurring. Congestion is defined as a state of network elements (such as switching nodes and transmission links) in which the network is not able to meet the negotiated performance objectives. Note that congestion is to be distinguished from queue saturation, which may happen while still remaining within the negotiated performance objective.

In a digital circuit switched telephone network, the admission control problem is to find an unused circuit on a route from source to destination for a single type of traffic. If a 64 kbit/s circuit is not available, then the connection is blocked. In ATM the problem is rather more complicated: not only must the route be found, but also a check must be made at each link on a proposed route to ensure that the new connection, with whatever traffic characteristics, can be supported without violating the negotiated performance requirements of connections established over each link.

In this chapter we focus on how we may make the check on each link, by making use of the cell scale and burst scale queueing analysis of previous chapters.

8.1 THE TRAFFIC CONTRACT

How are the bandwidth and performance requirements of the traffic contract specified? In our burst scale analysis so far, we have seen that there are three traffic parameters which are important in determining the type of queueing behaviour: peak cell rate, mean cell rate, and the average active state duration. For the performance requirement, we have concentrated on cell loss probability, but cell delay and CDV can also be important, particularly for interactive services.

The number of bandwidth parameters in the traffic contract is closely related to the complexity of the CAC algorithm and the type of queueing behaviour that is being permitted on the network. The simplest approach is CAC based on peak cell rate only: this limits the combined peak cell rate of all VCs through a buffer to less than or equal to the service capacity of the buffer. In this case there is never any burst scale queueing, so the CAC algorithm is based on cell scale queueing analysis. The ITU standards terminology for a traffic control framework based on peak cell rate only is "deterministic bit-rate (DBR) transfer capability".

If we add another bandwidth parameter, the mean cell rate, to the traffic contract and allow the peak cell rate to exceed the service capacity, this is one form of what is called the "statistical bit-rate (SBR) transfer capability" (see ITU Recommendation I.371 TRAFFIC CONTROL AND CONGESTION CONTROL IN B-ISDN, frozen issue — Geneva, July 1995). In this case the CAC algorithm is based on both cell scale queueing analysis and burst scale loss factor analysis (for reasons explained in the previous chapter), with buffers dimensioned to cope with cell scale queueing behaviour only.

Adding a third bandwidth parameter to quantify the burst length, allows another form of statistical bit-rate capability. This assumes buffers are large enough to cope with burst scale queueing, and the CAC algorithm is additionally based on analysis of the burst scale delay factor. Note that specifying SBR or DBR capability does not imply a particular choice of queueing analysis; it just means that the CAC algorithm is required to address both burst scale and cell scale queueing components (in the case of SBR) or just the cell scale queueing component (in the case of DBR). Likewise, the bandwidth parameters required in the traffic contract may depend on what analysis is employed (particularly for burst scale queueing).

However, it is universally accepted that the first step for operators of ATM networks is to provide the deterministic bit-rate transfer capability based on a single bandwidth parameter, the peak cell rate.

8.2 ADMISSIBLE LOAD: THE CELL SCALE CONSTRAINT

Let's say we have dimensioned a buffer to be 40 cells' capacity for a cell loss limit of 10^{-10} and a load of 75% (see Figure 6.4). We could make our maximum admissible load 75%, and not accept any more traffic if the extra load would increase the total beyond 75%. But what if the cell loss requirement is not so stringent? In this case the admissible load could be greater than 75%. Some straightforward manipulation of the heavy load approximation for the $M/D/1$ system (see Chapter 6) gives:

$$\rho = \frac{2x}{2x - \ln(\text{CLP})}$$

where we have the maximum admissible load defined in terms of the buffer capacity and the cell loss probability requirement.

A CAC algorithm based on M/D/1 analysis

How do we use this equation in a CAC algorithm? The traffic contract is based on just two parameters: the peak cell rate, h_i, and the required cell loss probability CLP_i, where $i = 1, 2, \ldots, n$, denotes the set of connections which have already been accepted and are currently in progress, i.e. they have not yet been cleared. Connection $n + 1$ is that request which is currently being tested. This connection is accepted if the following inequality holds:

$$\frac{h_{n+1}}{C} + \sum_{i=1}^{n} \frac{h_i}{C} \leqslant \frac{2x}{2x - \ln\left(\min_{i=1 \to n+1}(\text{CLP}_i)\right)}$$

where C is the bandwidth capacity of the link. Obviously it is not necessary to perform a summation of the peak rates every time because this can be recorded in a current load variable which is modified whenever a new connection is accepted or an existing connection is cleared. Similarly, a temporary variable holding the most stringent (i.e. the minimum) cell loss probability can be updated whenever a newly accepted connection has a lower CLP. However care must be taken to ensure that the minimum CLP is recomputed when calls are cleared, so that the performance requirements are based on the current set of accepted connections.

It is important to realise that the cell loss probability is suffered by all admitted connections, because all cells go through the one link in question. Hence the minimum CLP is the one which will give the most stringent limit on the admitted load, and it is this value which is used in the CAC formula. (This is in fact an approximation; different VCs passing through the same "first-come first-served" link buffer can suffer different cell loss probabilities depending on their particular traffic characteristics, but the variation is not large, and the analysis is complicated). Priority mechanisms can be used to distinguish between levels of CLP requirements; we deal with this in Chapter 11.

We know that the inequality is based on a heavy traffic approximation. For a buffer size of 40 cells and a CLP requirement of 10^{-10}, the equation gives a maximum admissible load of 77.65%, slightly higher than the 75% maximum obtained using the exact analysis. An alternative approach is to use look-up tables based on exact analysis instead of the expression on the right hand side of the inequality. Table 8.1 shows such a table, giving the maximum percentage load that can be admitted for finite buffer sizes ranging from five cells up to 100 cells, and cell loss probabilities ranging from 10^{-1} down to 10^{-10}. This table is generated by iteration of the output buffer analysis of Chapter 5 with Poisson input traffic.

A CAC algorithm based on ND/D/1 analysis

But what if all the traffic is CBR and the number of sources is relatively small? We know from the $ND/D/1$ analysis that the admissible load can be greater than that given by the $M/D/1$ results for a given CLP requirement. The problem with the $ND/D/1$ analysis is that it models a homogeneous source mix, i.e. all sources have the same traffic characteristics. In general, this will not be the case. However, it turns out that for a fixed load, ρ, and a constant number of sources, N, the worst case situation for cell loss is the homogeneous case. Thus we can use the $ND/D/1$ results and apply them in the general situation where there are N sources of different peak cell rates.

Table 8.1
CAC look-up table for finite M/D/1: admissible load (%), given buffer capacity and cell loss probability (10^{-1} to 10^{-12})

x (cells)	Cell loss probability											
	10^{-1}	10^{-2}	10^{-3}	10^{-4}	10^{-5}	10^{-6}	10^{-7}	10^{-8}	10^{-9}	10^{-10}	10^{-11}	10^{-12}
5	96.3	59.7	41.9	16.6	6.6	2.9	1.35	0.62	0.28	0.13	0.06	0.03
10	99.9	85.2	71.2	60.1	50.7	42.7	35.8	29.9	24.9	20.7	17.1	14.2
15	99.9	92.4	82.4	74.2	66.9	60.4	54.4	49.0	44.0	39.5	35.4	31.6
20	99.9	95.6	87.7	81.3	75.5	70.2	65.2	60.5	56.2	52.1	48.2	44.6
25	99.9	97.2	90.7	85.4	80.7	76.2	72.0	68.0	64.2	60.6	57.2	53.9
30	99.9	98.2	92.7	88.2	84.1	80.3	76.7	73.2	69.9	66.7	63.6	60.7
35	99.9	98.9	94.0	90.1	86.6	83.2	80.0	77.0	74.0	71.2	68.4	65.8
40	99.9	99.4	95.0	91.5	88.4	85.4	82.6	79.8	77.2	74.6	72.1	69.7
45	99.9	99.7	95.7	92.6	89.8	87.1	84.6	82.1	79.7	77.4	75.1	72.9
50	99.9	99.9	96.3	93.5	90.9	88.5	86.2	83.9	81.7	79.6	77.5	75.5
55	99.9	99.9	96.7	94.2	91.8	89.6	87.5	85.4	83.4	81.4	79.5	77.6
60	99.9	99.9	97.1	94.7	92.6	90.5	88.6	86.7	84.8	83.0	81.2	79.4
65	99.9	99.9	97.4	95.2	93.2	91.3	89.5	87.7	86.0	84.3	82.6	81.0
70	99.9	99.9	97.7	95.6	93.7	92.0	90.3	88.6	87.0	85.4	83.8	82.3
75	99.9	99.9	97.9	95.9	94.2	92.5	91.0	89.4	87.9	86.4	84.9	83.5
80	99.9	99.9	98.1	96.2	94.6	93.0	91.5	90.1	88.6	87.2	85.9	84.5
85	99.9	99.9	98.2	96.5	95.0	93.5	92.1	90.7	89.3	88.0	86.7	85.4
90	99.9	99.9	98.4	96.7	95.3	93.9	92.5	91.2	89.9	88.7	87.4	86.2
95	99.9	99.9	98.5	96.9	95.5	94.2	92.9	91.7	90.5	89.3	88.1	86.9
100	99.9	99.9	98.6	97.1	95.8	94.5	93.3	92.1	91.0	89.8	88.7	87.6

As for the $M/D/1$ system, we manipulate the heavy load approximation for the $ND/D/1$ queue by taking logs of both sides, and rearrange in terms of ρ

$$\text{CLP} = \exp\left[-2x\left(\frac{x}{N} + \frac{1-\rho}{\rho}\right)\right]$$

which gives the formula

$$\rho = \frac{2xN}{2xN - (2x^2 + N\ln(\text{CLP}))}$$

It is possible for this formula to return values of admissible load greater than 100%, specifically when

$$2x^2 + N\ln(\text{CLP}) > 0$$

Such a load would obviously take the queue into a permanent (burst scale) overload, causing significantly more cell loss than that specified. However, it does provide us with a first test for a CAC algorithm based on this analysis, i.e. if

$$n + 1 \leqslant -\frac{2x^2}{\ln\left(\min_{i=1\to n+1}(\text{CLP}_i)\right)}$$

then we can load the link up to 100% with any mix of $n+1$ CBR sources, i.e. we can accept the connection provided that

$$\frac{h_{n+1}}{C} + \sum_{i=1}^{n}\frac{h_i}{C} \leqslant 1$$

Otherwise, if

$$n + 1 > -\frac{2x^2}{\ln\left(\min_{i=1\to n+1}(\text{CLP}_i)\right)}$$

then we can accept the connection if

$$\frac{h_{n+1}}{C} + \sum_{i=1}^{n}\frac{h_i}{C} \leqslant \frac{2x(n+1)}{2x(n+1) - \left[2x^2 + (n+1)\ln\left(\min_{i=1\to n+1}(\text{CLP}_i)\right)\right]}$$

It is also important to remember that the $ND/D/1$ analysis is only required when $N > x$. If there are fewer sources than buffer places, then the queue never overflows, and so the admissible load is 100%.

Like the $M/D/1$ system, this inequality is based on a heavy load approximation. A look-up table method based on iteration of the equation:

$$\text{CLP} \approx \sum_{n=x+1}^{N} \left\{ \frac{N!}{n!(N-n)!} \left(\frac{n-x}{D}\right)^n \left[1 - \left(\frac{n-x}{D}\right)\right]^{N-n} \frac{D-N+x}{D-n+x} \right\}$$

provides a *better* approximation than the heavy load approximation, but note that it is not an exact analysis as in Table 8.1 for the finite $M/D/1$.

The approach is more complicated than for the $M/D/1$ system because of the dependence on a third parameter, N. Table 8.2 shows the maximum number of sources admissible for a load of 100%, for combinations of buffer capacity and cell loss probability. Table 8.3 then shows the maximum admissible load for combinations of N and cell loss probability, in three parts: (a) for a buffer capacity of 10 cells; (b) for 50 cells; (c) for 100 cells.

The tables are used as follows: first check if the number of sources is less than that given by Table 8.2 for a given CLP and buffer capacity; if so, then the admissible load is 100%. Otherwise, use the appropriate part of Table 8.3, with the given number of sources and CLP requirement, to find the maximum admissible load. Note that when the maximum admissible load is less than 100% of the cell rate capacity of the link, the bandwidth that is effectively being allocated to each source is greater than the source's peak cell rate, h_i. This allocated bandwidth is found simply by dividing the peak cell rate of a source by the maximum admissible load (expressed as a fraction, not as a percentage).

This CAC algorithm, based on either the $ND/D/1$ approximate analysis, or the associated tables, is appropriate for the deterministic bit-rate capability. The parameters required are just the peak (cell) rate h_i, and the required cell loss probability, CLP_i, for each source i, along with the buffer capacity x, the cell rate capacity C, and the number of connections currently in progress, n. Note that it is acceptable when using the deterministic bit-rate capability, to mix variable and constant bit-rate sources, provided that the peak cell rate of a source is used in calculating the allocated load. The important point is that it is only the peak cell rate which is used to characterise the source's traffic behaviour.

The cell scale constraint in statistical bit-rate capability, based on M/D/1 analysis

A cell-scale constraint is also a component of the CAC algorithm for the statistical bit-rate capability. Here, the $M/D/1$ system is more appropriate, using the mean cell rate, m_i, instead of the peak cell rate

Table 8.2
CAC look-up table for deterministic bit-rate transfer capability: maximum number of sources for 100% loading, given buffer capacity and cell loss probability (10^{-1} to 10^{-12})

x (cells)	10^{-1}	10^{-2}	10^{-3}	10^{-4}	10^{-5}	10^{-6}	10^{-7}	10^{-8}	10^{-9}	10^{-10}	10^{-11}	10^{-12}
5	23	11	8	6	5	5	5	5	5	5	5	5
10	89	45	30	23	19	16	14	13	12	11	11	10
15	200	100	67	50	41	34	30	26	24	22	20	19
20	353	176	118	89	71	60	52	45	41	37	34	32
25	550	275	183	138	111	92	80	70	63	57	52	48
30	790	395	264	198	159	133	114	100	89	81	74	68
35	1064	537	358	269	215	180	155	136	121	109	100	92
40	1389	701	467	351	281	234	201	176	157	142	129	119
45	1758	886	591	443	355	296	254	223	198	179	163	150
50	2171	1085	729	547	438	365	313	275	244	220	201	185
55	2627	1313	881	661	529	441	379	332	295	266	242	223
60	3126	1563	1042	786	629	525	450	394	351	316	288	264
65	3669	1834	1223	922	738	616	528	462	411	371	337	310
70	4256	2128	1418	1064	856	714	612	536	477	429	391	359
75	4885	2442	1628	1221	982	819	702	615	547	493	448	411
80	5558	2779	1852	1389	1111	931	799	699	622	560	510	468
85	6275	3137	2091	1568	1255	1045	901	789	702	632	575	527
90	7035	3517	2345	1758	1407	1172	1005	884	786	708	644	591
95	7839	3919	2613	1959	1567	1306	1119	985	876	788	717	658
100	8685	4342	2895	2171	1737	1447	1240	1085	970	873	794	729

Cell loss probability

Table 8.3(a)

Maximum admissible load (%) for a buffer capacity of 10 cells, given number of sources and cell loss probability (10^{-1} to 10^{-12})

N						Cell loss probability						
	10^{-1}	10^{-2}	10^{-3}	10^{-4}	10^{-5}	10^{-6}	10^{-7}	10^{-8}	10^{-9}	10^{-10}	10^{-11}	10^{-12}
10	100.0	100.0	100.0	100.0	100.0	100.0	100.0	100.0	100.0	100.0	100.0	100.0
11	100.0	100.0	100.0	100.0	100.0	100.0	100.0	100.0	100.0	100.0	100.0	84.6
12	100.0	100.0	100.0	100.0	100.0	100.0	100.0	100.0	100.0	85.7	70.6	57.1
13	100.0	100.0	100.0	100.0	100.0	100.0	100.0	100.0	81.3	68.4	59.1	48.2
14	100.0	100.0	100.0	100.0	100.0	100.0	100.0	87.5	73.7	60.9	51.9	42.4
15	100.0	100.0	100.0	100.0	100.0	100.0	93.8	79.0	65.2	55.6	46.9	39.5
16	100.0	100.0	100.0	100.0	100.0	100.0	84.2	72.7	61.5	51.6	43.2	36.4
17	100.0	100.0	100.0	100.0	100.0	94.4	81.0	68.0	56.7	48.6	41.5	34.7
18	100.0	100.0	100.0	100.0	100.0	85.7	75.0	64.3	54.6	46.2	39.1	33.3
19	100.0	100.0	100.0	100.0	100.0	82.6	73.1	61.3	52.8	44.2	38.0	32.2
20	100.0	100.0	100.0	100.0	95.2	80.0	69.0	58.8	50.0	42.6	36.4	30.8
30	100.0	100.0	88.9	85.7	75.0	65.2	56.6	48.4	41.7	35.7	30.3	25.9
40	100.0	96.2	84.8	78.4	69.0	59.7	51.3	44.4	38.1	32.8	28.0	24.0
50	100.0	93.8	82.2	74.6	64.9	56.8	49.0	42.4	36.5	31.5	26.9	22.9
60	100.0	90.9	80.5	72.3	63.2	55.1	47.6	41.1	35.5	30.5	26.1	22.3
70	100.0	88.9	78.4	70.7	61.4	53.9	46.7	40.5	34.8	29.9	25.6	21.9
80	100.0	88.2	77.6	69.0	60.6	53.0	46.0	39.8	34.3	29.5	25.3	21.6
90	98.9	87.0	76.9	68.2	60.0	52.3	45.5	39.3	34.0	29.2	25.0	21.3
100	98.0	83.0	73.5	67.6	59.2	51.8	44.8	38.9	33.7	28.9	24.8	21.2
200	93.5	81.7	72.3	64.7	56.7	49.5	43.1	37.4	32.3	27.9	23.9	20.5
300	92.0	81.1	71.8	63.7	56.0	48.9	42.6	37.0	31.9	27.5	23.6	20.2
400	91.3	80.8	71.6	63.3	55.6	48.5	42.3	36.7	31.7	27.3	23.5	20.1
500	90.9	80.5	71.5	63.1	55.3	48.4	42.1	36.6	31.6	27.3	23.4	20.0
600	90.6	80.4	71.4	62.8	55.2	48.2	42.0	36.5	31.6	27.2	23.3	20.0
700	90.4	80.2	71.2	62.7	55.1	48.1	41.9	36.4	31.5	27.1	23.3	20.0
800	90.3	80.1	71.1	62.6	55.0	48.1	41.9	36.4	31.5	27.1	23.3	19.9
900	90.2	80.1	71.0	62.5	54.9	48.0	41.8	36.3	31.4	27.1	23.3	19.9
1000	90.1	80.1	71.0	62.5	54.9	48.0	41.8	36.3	31.4	27.1	23.2	19.9

Table 8.3(b)

Maximum admissible load (%) for a buffer capacity of 50 cells, given number of sources and cell loss probability (10^{-1} to 10^{-12})

N	10^{-1}	10^{-2}	10^{-3}	10^{-4}	10^{-5}	10^{-6}	10^{-7}	10^{-8}	10^{-9}	10^{-10}	10^{-11}	10^{-12}
						Cell loss probability						
180	100.0	100.0	100.0	100.0	100.0	100.0	100.0	100.0	100.0	100.0	100.0	100.0
190	100.0	100.0	100.0	100.0	100.0	100.0	100.0	100.0	100.0	100.0	100.0	99.0
200	100.0	100.0	100.0	100.0	100.0	100.0	100.0	100.0	100.0	100.0	100.0	97.1
210	100.0	100.0	100.0	100.0	100.0	100.0	100.0	100.0	100.0	100.0	98.6	95.9
220	100.0	100.0	100.0	100.0	100.0	100.0	100.0	100.0	100.0	100.0	97.4	94.8
240	100.0	100.0	100.0	100.0	100.0	100.0	100.0	100.0	100.0	97.6	95.2	92.7
260	100.0	100.0	100.0	100.0	100.0	100.0	100.0	100.0	98.5	95.9	93.5	90.9
280	100.0	100.0	100.0	100.0	100.0	100.0	100.0	99.3	96.9	94.6	92.1	89.7
300	100.0	100.0	100.0	100.0	100.0	100.0	100.0	98.0	95.5	93.2	90.9	88.5
350	100.0	100.0	100.0	100.0	100.0	100.0	98.0	95.6	93.1	90.9	88.6	86.2
400	100.0	100.0	100.0	100.0	100.0	98.5	96.2	93.9	91.5	89.1	87.0	84.8
450	100.0	100.0	100.0	100.0	99.6	97.2	94.7	92.4	90.2	87.9	85.7	83.5
500	100.0	100.0	100.0	100.0	98.4	96.0	93.6	91.4	89.1	87.0	84.8	82.5
550	100.0	100.0	100.0	99.8	97.5	95.2	92.8	90.5	88.3	86.1	84.0	81.9
600	100.0	100.0	100.0	99.0	96.6	94.3	92.0	89.8	87.6	85.5	83.3	81.2
700	100.0	100.0	100.0	97.9	95.5	93.2	90.9	88.7	86.5	84.4	82.4	80.3
800	100.0	100.0	99.3	97.0	94.7	92.4	90.2	87.9	85.8	83.7	81.6	79.6
900	100.0	100.0	98.6	96.3	94.0	91.7	89.6	87.4	85.2	83.1	81.1	79.0
1000	100.0	100.0	98.1	95.7	93.5	91.2	89.1	86.9	84.8	82.6	80.7	78.6

Table 8.3(c)
Maximum admissible load (%) for a buffer capacity of 100 cells

N	Cell loss probability				
	10^{-8}	10^{-9}	10^{-10}	10^{-11}	10^{-12}
700	100.0	100.0	100.0	100.0	100.0
750	100.0	100.0	100.0	100.0	99.5
800	100.0	100.0	100.0	99.9	98.6
850	100.0	100.0	100.0	99.1	97.8
900	100.0	100.0	99.6	98.4	97.2
950	100.0	100.0	99.0	97.7	96.5
1000	100.0	99.6	98.4	97.2	96.0

h_i, to calculate the load in the inequality test; i.e. if

$$\frac{m_{n+1}}{C} + \sum_{i=1}^{n} \frac{m_i}{C} \leqslant \frac{2x}{2x - \ln\left(\min_{i=1\to n+1}(\text{CLP}_i)\right)}$$

is satisfied, then the cell-scale behaviour is within the required cell loss probability limits, and the CAC algorithm must then check the burst-scale constraint before making an accept/reject decision. If the inequality is not satisfied, then the connection can immediately be rejected. For a more accurate test, values from the look-up table in Table 8.1 can be used instead of the expression on the right hand side of the inequality.

8.3 ADMISSIBLE LOAD: THE BURST SCALE

Let's now look at the loads which can be accepted for bursty sources. For this we will use the burst scale loss analysis of the previous chapter, i.e. assume that the buffer is of zero size at the burst scale. Remember that each source has an average rate of m cell/s, so with N sources, the utilisation is given by

$$\rho = \frac{Nm}{C}$$

Unfortunately we do not have a simple approximate formula that can be manipulated to give the admissible load as an explicit function of the traffic contract parameters. The best we can do to simplify the situation is to use the approximate formula for the burst scale loss factor:

$$\text{CLP} \approx \frac{1}{(1-\rho)^2 N_0} \cdot \frac{(\rho N_0)^{\lfloor N_0 \rfloor}}{\lfloor N_0 \rfloor !} e^{-\rho N_0}$$

How can we use this formula in a connection admission control algorithm? In a similar manner to Erlang's lost call formula, we must use the formula to produce a table which allows us, in this case, to specify the required cell loss probability and the source peak cell rate and find out the maximum allowed utilisation. We can then calculate the maximum number of sources of this type (with mean cell rate m) that can be accepted using the formula

$$N = \frac{\rho C}{m}$$

Table 8.4 does not directly use the peak cell rate, but rather the number of peak cell rates which fit into the service capacity, i.e. the parameter N_0. Example peak rates for the standard service capacity of 353 208 cell/s are shown.

So, if we have a source with a peak cell rate of 8830.19 cell/s (i.e. 3.39 Mbit/s) and a mean cell rate of 2000 cell/s (i.e. 768 kbit/s), and we want the CLP to be no more than 10^{-10}, then we can accept

$$N = \frac{0.332 \times 353\,208}{2000} = 58.63$$

i.e. 58 connections of this type. This is 18 more connections than if we had used the deterministic bit-rate capability (assuming 100% allocation of peak rates, which is possible if the buffer capacity is 25 cells or more). The ratio

$$G = \frac{N}{N_0}$$

is called the statistical multiplexing gain. This is the actual number accepted, N, divided by the number N_0 if we were to allocate on the peak rate only. It gives an indication of how much better the utilisation is when using SBR capability compared with using DBR capability. If peak rate allocation is used, then there is no statistical multiplexing gain, and G is 1.

But what happens if there are different types of source? If all the sources have the same peak cell rate, then the actual mean rates of individual sources do not matter, so long as the total mean cell rate is less than ρC, i.e.

$$\sum_i m_i \leqslant \rho C$$

Table 8.4
Maximum admissible load (%) for burst scale constraint

h (cell/s)	N_0	Cell loss probability											
		10^{-1}	10^{-2}	10^{-3}	10^{-4}	10^{-5}	10^{-6}	10^{-7}	10^{-8}	10^{-9}	10^{-10}	10^{-11}	10^{-12}
35 320.76	10	72.1	52.3	37.9	28.1	21.2	16.2	12.5	9.7	7.6	5.9	4.7	3.7
17 660.38	20	82.3	67.0	54.3	44.9	37.7	32.0	27.4	23.6	20.5	17.8	15.6	13.6
11 773.59	30	86.5	73.7	62.5	53.8	46.9	41.4	36.8	32.9	29.6	26.7	24.1	21.9
8830.19	40	88.9	77.8	67.5	59.5	53.0	47.7	43.3	39.4	36.1	33.2	30.6	28.2
7064.15	50	90.5	80.5	71.1	63.5	57.4	52.4	48.1	44.3	41.1	38.2	35.6	33.2
5886.79	60	91.7	82.5	73.7	66.6	60.8	55.9	51.8	48.2	45.0	42.2	39.6	37.3
5045.82	70	92.5	84.1	75.8	69.0	63.5	58.8	54.8	51.3	48.3	45.5	43.0	40.7
4415.09	80	93.2	85.3	77.4	71.0	65.7	61.2	57.3	54.0	51.0	48.3	45.8	43.6
3924.53	90	93.7	86.3	78.8	72.6	67.5	63.2	59.5	56.2	53.3	50.6	48.2	46.0
3532.08	100	94.2	87.2	80.0	74.0	69.1	64.9	61.3	58.1	55.3	52.7	50.4	48.2
1766.04	200	96.4	91.7	86.4	81.8	78.0	74.7	71.8	69.3	67.0	64.9	62.9	61.1
1177.36	300	97.3	93.6	89.2	85.3	82.0	79.2	76.8	74.6	72.6	70.7	69.0	67.5
883.02	400	97.8	94.7	90.8	87.4	84.5	82.0	79.8	77.8	76.0	74.4	72.8	71.4
706.42	500	98.1	95.4	91.9	88.8	86.2	83.9	81.9	80.1	78.4	76.9	75.5	74.2
588.68	600	98.4	95.9	92.7	89.9	87.4	85.3	83.4	81.8	80.2	78.8	77.5	76.3
504.58	700	98.5	96.3	93.3	90.7	88.4	86.4	84.7	83.1	81.7	80.3	79.1	78.0

So, the connection is accepted if the following inequality holds:

$$\frac{m_{n+1}}{C} + \sum_{i=1}^{n} \frac{m_i}{C} \leqslant \rho(\text{CLP}, N_0)$$

where ρ is chosen (as a function of CLP and N_0) from Table 8.4 in the manner described previously.

A practical CAC scheme

Notice in the table that the value of ρ decreases as the peak cell rate increases. We could therefore use this approach in a more conservative way by choosing ρ according to the most stringent (i.e. highest) peak rate source in the mix. This is effectively assuming that all sources, whatever their mean rate, have a peak rate equal to the highest in the traffic mix. The CAC algorithm would need to keep track of this maximum peak rate (as well as the minimum CLP requirement), and update the admissible load accordingly. The inequality test for this scheme is therefore written as:

$$\frac{m_{n+1}}{C} + \sum_{i=1}^{n} \frac{m_i}{C} \leqslant \rho \left(\min_{i=1 \to n+1} (\text{CLP}_i), \frac{C}{\max\limits_{i=1 \to n+1} (h_i)} \right)$$

Equivalent cell rate and linear CAC

A different approach is to think in terms of the cell rate allocated to a source. For the DBR capability, a CAC algorithm allocates either the source's peak cell rate or a value *greater* than this, because cell scale queueing limits the admissible load. This keeps the utilisation, defined in terms of peak rates, at or below 100%. With SBR capability, the total *peak* rate allocated can be in excess of 100%, so the actual portion of service capacity allocated to a source is below the peak cell rate (and, necessarily, above the mean cell rate). This allocation is called the *equivalent cell rate*.

Other terms have been used to describe essentially the same concept: effective bandwidth and equivalent capacity are the most common terms used, but the precise definition is usually associated with a particular analytical method. Equivalent cell rate is the term used in the ITU standards documents.

The key contribution made by the concept of equivalent cell rate is the idea of a single value to represent the amount of resource required for a single source in a traffic mix at a given CLP requirement. This makes the admission control process simply a matter of adding the equivalent cell rate of the requested connection to the currently allocated value. If it exceeds the service rate available then the request is rejected. This is an attractive approach for traffic mixes of different types of sources because of its apparent simplicity. It is known as "linear CAC".

The difficulty lies in defining the equivalent cell rate for a particular source type. The issue rests on how well different types of sources are able to mix when multiplexed through the same buffer. The analysis we have used so far is for a traffic mix of sources of the same type. In this case, the equivalent cell rate can be defined as

$$\text{ECR} = \frac{C}{N} = \frac{h}{G}$$

When the statistical multiplexing gain G is low (i.e. approaching a value of 1), the equivalent cell rate approaches the peak rate of the source and the cell loss probability will be low. Conversely, when the gain is high, the equivalent cell rate approaches the mean rate of the source, and the cell loss probability is high.

Equivalent cell rate based on a traffic mix of sources of the same type may underestimate the resources required when sources of very different characteristics are present. The exact analysis of heterogeneous source multiplexing is beyond the scope of this book, but there are other approaches.

Two level CAC

One of these approaches, aimed at simplifying CAC, is to divide the sources into classes and partition the service capacity so that each source class is allocated a proportion of it. The homogeneous source analysis can be justified in this case because the fraction of service rate allocated to the *class* is used instead of the total service capacity (within the fraction, all the sources are the same). This has the effect of reducing N_0, and hence reducing the admissible load per class. The problem with this approach is that a connection of one type may be rejected if its allocation is full, even though there is unused capacity because other service classes are underused.

A solution is to divide the CAC algorithm into two levels. The first level makes accept/reject decisions by comparing the current service class allocations with the maximum number allowed. But this is supported by a second level "back-room" task which redistributes unused capacity to service classes that need it. The second level is computationally intensive because it must ensure that the allocations it proposes conform to the required cell loss probability. This takes time, and so the allocations are updated on a (relatively) longer timescale. However, the first level is a very simple comparison and so a connection request can be assessed immediately.

The basic principle of the two level scheme is to have a first level which can make an instant decision on a connection request, and a second level which can perform detailed traffic calculations in the background to keep the scheme as accurate as possible. The service class approach is just one of many: other algorithms for the first and second levels have been proposed in the literature.

Accounting for the burst scale delay factor

Whatever the size of buffer, large or small, the actual burst scale loss depends on the two burst scale factors: the loss factor assumes there is no buffer, and the delay factor quantifies how much less is the loss if we incorporate buffering. Thus, if we use the loss factor only, we will tend to overestimate the cell loss; or for a fixed CLP, we will underestimate the admissible load.

So, for small buffer capacities, just using the loss factor is a good starting point for admission control at the burst scale. But we have already incorporated some "conservative" assumptions into our practical scheme, and even small buffers can produce some useful gains under certain circumstances. How can the scheme be modified to account for the burst scale delay factor, and hence increase the admissible load?

Let's use our previous example of 58 connections (peak cell rate 8830.19 cell/s, mean cell rate 2000 cell/s, $N_0 = 40$, and a CLP of 10^{-10}) and see how many more connections can be accepted if the average burst duration is 40 ms and the buffer capacity is 475 cells. First, we need to calculate:

$$\frac{N_0 x}{b} = \frac{40 \times 475}{0.04 \times 8830.19} = 53.79$$

and the admissible load (from the burst scale loss analysis) is

$$\rho = \frac{58 \times 2000}{353\,208} = 0.328$$

So we can calculate the CLP gain due to the burst scale delay factor:

$$\mathrm{CLP}_{\text{excess-rate}} = \exp\left[-N_0 \frac{x}{b} \frac{(1-\rho)^3}{4\rho + 1}\right] = 8.58 \times 10^{-4}$$

Table 8.5
Burst scale delay factor table for values of N_0x/b, given admissible load and CLP (10^{-1} to 10^{-12})

Load, ρ	10^{-1}	10^{-2}	10^{-3}	10^{-4}	10^{-5}	Cell loss probability 10^{-6}	10^{-7}	10^{-8}	10^{-9}	10^{-10}	10^{-11}	10^{-12}
0.02	2.6	5.3	7.9	10.6	13.2	15.9	18.5	21.1	23.8	26.4	29.1	31.7
0.04	3.0	6.0	9.1	12.1	15.1	18.1	21.1	24.2	27.2	30.2	33.2	36.2
0.06	3.4	6.9	10.3	13.8	17.2	20.6	24.1	27.5	30.9	34.4	37.8	41.3
0.08	3.9	7.8	11.7	15.6	19.5	23.4	27.3	31.2	35.1	39.0	42.9	46.8
0.10	4.4	8.8	13.3	17.7	22.1	26.5	31.0	35.4	39.8	44.2	48.6	53.1
0.12	5.0	10.0	15.0	20.0	25.0	30.0	35.0	40.0	45.0	50.0	55.0	60.0
0.14	5.6	11.3	16.9	22.6	28.2	33.9	39.5	45.2	50.8	56.5	62.1	67.8
0.16	6.4	12.7	19.1	25.5	31.9	38.2	44.6	51.0	57.3	63.7	70.1	76.5
0.18	7.2	14.4	21.5	28.7	35.9	43.1	50.3	57.5	64.6	71.8	79.0	86.2
0.20	8.1	16.2	24.3	32.4	40.5	48.6	56.7	64.8	72.9	81.0	89.0	97.1
0.22	9.1	18.2	27.4	36.5	45.6	54.7	63.9	73.0	82.1	91.2	100.3	109.5
0.24	10.3	20.6	30.8	41.1	51.4	61.7	72.0	82.2	92.5	102.8	113.1	123.4
0.26	11.6	23.2	34.8	46.4	58.0	69.6	81.1	92.7	104.3	115.9	127.5	139.1
0.28	13.1	26.2	39.2	52.3	65.4	78.5	91.5	104.6	117.7	130.8	143.9	156.9
0.30	14.8	29.5	44.3	59.1	73.8	88.6	103.4	118.2	132.9	147.7	162.5	177.2
0.32	16.7	33.4	50.1	66.8	83.5	100.2	116.9	133.6	150.3	167.0	183.7	200.4
0.34	18.9	37.8	56.7	75.6	94.5	113.4	132.3	151.2	170.1	189.0	207.9	226.8
0.36	21.4	42.9	64.3	85.7	107.2	128.6	150.0	171.5	192.9	214.3	235.8	257.2
0.38	24.3	48.7	73.0	97.4	121.7	146.1	170.4	194.8	219.1	243.5	267.8	292.2
0.40	27.7	55.4	83.1	110.9	138.6	166.3	194.0	221.7	249.4	277.2	304.9	332.6
0.42	31.6	63.3	94.9	126.5	158.1	189.8	221.4	253.0	284.6	316.3	347.9	379.5
0.44	36.2	72.4	108.6	144.8	180.9	217.1	253.3	289.5	325.7	361.9	398.1	434.3
0.46	41.5	83.1	124.6	166.1	207.6	249.2	290.7	332.2	373.8	415.3	456.8	498.3
0.48	47.8	95.6	143.5	191.3	239.1	286.9	334.7	382.5	430.4	478.2	526.0	573.8
0.50	55.3	110.5	165.8	221.0	276.3	331.6	386.8	442.1	497.4	552.6	607.9	663.1
0.52	64.1	128.3	192.4	256.5	320.6	384.8	448.9	513.0	577.1	641.3	705.4	769.5
0.54	74.8	149.5	224.3	299.0	373.8	448.5	523.3	598.0	672.8	747.5	822.3	897.0

continued overleaf

Table 8.5 (*continued*)

Load, ρ	10^{-1}	10^{-2}	10^{-3}	10^{-4}	10^{-5}	10^{-6}	10^{-7}	10^{-8}	10^{-9}	10^{-10}	10^{-11}	10^{-12}
						Cell loss probability						
0.56	87.6	175.2	262.7	350.3	437.9	525.5	613.1	700.6	788.2	875.8	963.4	1051.0
0.58	103.2	206.4	309.5	412.7	515.9	619.1	722.3	825.5	928.6	1031.8	1135.0	1238.2
0.60	122.3	244.6	367.0	489.3	611.6	733.9	856.3	978.6	1100.9	1223.2	1345.6	1467.9
0.62	146.0	292.1	438.1	584.1	730.2	876.2	1022.2	1168.2	1314.3	1460.3	1606.3	1752.4
0.64	175.7	351.4	527.1	702.8	878.5	1054.2	1229.9	1405.6	1581.3	1756.9	1932.6	2108.3
0.66	213.2	426.5	639.7	853.0	1066.2	1279.5	1492.7	1706.0	1919.2	2132.5	2345.7	2558.9
0.68	261.4	522.8	784.2	1045.6	1307.0	1568.4	1829.8	2091.2	2352.6	2614.0	2875.4	3136.8
0.70	324.1	648.1	972.2	1296.3	1620.3	1944.4	2268.5	2592.5	2916.6	3240.7	3564.7	3888.8
0.72	407.0	814.0	1220.9	1627.9	2034.9	2441.9	2848.9	3255.8	3662.8	4069.8	4476.8	4883.8
0.74	518.8	1037.6	1556.4	2075.2	2593.9	3112.7	3631.5	4150.3	4669.1	5187.9	5706.7	6225.5
0.76	672.9	1345.8	2018.8	2691.7	3364.6	4037.5	4710.4	5383.4	6056.3	6729.2	7402.1	8075.0
0.78	890.9	1781.9	2672.8	3563.7	4454.7	5345.6	6236.5	7127.5	8018.4	8909.3	9800.3	10691.2
0.80	1208.9	2417.7	3626.6	4835.4	6044.3	7253.1	8462.0	9670.9	10879.7	12088.6	13297.4	14506.3
0.82	1689.8	3379.7	5069.5	6759.3	8449.1	10139.0	11828.8	13518.6	15208.4	16898.3	18588.1	20277.9
0.84	2451.0	4902.0	7353.0	9804.0	12255.0	14706.0	17157.0	19608.0	22058.9	24509.9	26960.9	29411.9
0.86	3725.8	7451.5	11177.3	14903.0	18628.8	22354.5	26080.3	29806.1	33531.8	37257.6	40983.3	44709.1
0.88	6023.0	12045.9	18068.9	24091.9	30114.8	36137.8	42160.8	48183.7	54206.7	60229.7	66252.6	72275.6
0.90	10591.9	21183.8	31775.7	42367.6	52959.5	63551.3	74143.2	84735.1	95327.0	105918.9	116510.8	127102.7
0.92	21047.1	42094.1	63141.2	84188.3	105235.3	126282.4	147329.5	168376.5	189423.6	210470.7	231517.7	252564.8
0.94	50742.2	101484.3	152226.5	202968.6	253710.8	304452.9	355195.1	405937.2	456679.4	507421.5	558163.7	608905.8
0.96	174133.0	348266.0	522399.0	696532.0	870665.0	1044798.0	1218931.0	1393064.0	1567197.0	1741330.0	1915463.0	2089596.0
0.98	1416089.8	2832179.7	4248269.5	5664359.3	7080449.2	8496539.0	9912628.8	11328718.7	12744808.5	14160898.3	15576988.2	16993078.0

Thus there is a further CLP gain of about 10^{-3}, i.e. an overall CLP of about 10^{-13}.

Although the excess-rate cell loss is an exponential function, which can thus be rearranged fairly easily, we will use a tabular approach because it clearly illustrates the process required. Table 8.5 specifies the CLP and the admissible load in order to find a value for $N_0 x/b$ (this was introduced in Chapter 7 as the size of a buffer in units of excess rate bursts). The CLP target is 10^{-10}. By how much can the load be increased so that the overall CLP meets this target? Looking down the 10^{-2} column of Table 8.5, we find that the admissible load could increase to a value of nearly 0.4. Then, we check in Table 8.4 to see that the burst scale loss contribution for a load of 0.394 is 10^{-8}. Thus the overall CLP meets our target of 10^{-10}.

The number of connections that can be accepted is now

$$N = \frac{0.394 \times 353\,208}{2000} = 69.58$$

i.e. 69 connections of this type. This is a further 11 connections more than if we had just used the burst scale loss factor as the basis for the CAC algorithm. The penalty is the increased size of the buffer, and the correspondingly greater delays incurred (about 1.3 ms maximum, for a buffer capacity of 475 cells). However, the example illustrates the principle, and even with buffers of less than 100 cells, worthwhile gains in admissible load are possible. The main difficulty with the process is in selecting a load to provide cell loss factors from Tables 8.4 and 8.5 which combine to the required target cell loss. The target cell loss can be found by trial and error, gradually reducing the excess rate CLP by taking the next column to the left in Table 8.5.

8.4 CAC IN THE STANDARDS

Connection admission control is defined in ITU Recommendation I.371 (TRAFFIC CONTROL AND CONGESTION CONTROL IN B-ISDN, frozen issue — Geneva, July 1995) as the set of actions taken by the network at the call set-up phase (or during call renegotiation) to establish whether a connection can be accepted or whether it must be rejected. We have seen that the CAC algorithm needs to know the source traffic characteristics and the required performance in order to determine whether the connection can be accepted or not and, if accepted, the amount of network resources to allocate. Also it must set the traffic parameters needed by usage parameter control — this will be addressed in the next chapter.

Recommendation I.371 does not specify any particular CAC algorithm; it merely observes that many CAC policies are possible, and it is up to the network operator to choose. A draft new recommendation E.73x (METHODS FOR TRAFFIC CONTROL IN B-ISDN, November 1995) outlines some possible policies. It distinguishes three different operating principles:

1.   Multiplexing of constant bit-rate streams
2.   Rate envelope multiplexing
3.   Rate sharing statistical multiplexing

The first corresponds to peak rate allocation, i.e. the deterministic bit-rate transfer capability, and deals with the cell scale queueing behaviour. In this book we have considered two different algorithms, based on either the $M/D/1$ or $ND/D/1$ systems. The second and third operating principles allow for the statistical multiplexing of variable bit-rate streams and are two approaches to providing the statistical bit-rate transfer capability. Rate envelope multiplexing is the term for what we have called the burst scale loss factor, i.e. it is the bufferless approach. The term arises because the objective is to keep the total input rate to within the service rate; any excess rate is assumed to be lost. Rate sharing corresponds to the combined burst scale loss and delay factors, i.e. it assumes there is a large buffer available to cope with the excess cell rates. It allows higher admissible loads, but the penalty is greater delay. Thus the objective is not to limit the combined cell rate, but to share the service capacity by providing sufficient buffer space to absorb the excess rate cells.

These three different operating principles require different traffic parameters to describe the source traffic characteristics. DBR requires just the peak cell rate of the source. Rate envelope multiplexing additionally needs the mean cell rate, and rate sharing requires peak cell rate, mean cell rate and some measure of burst length. The actual parameters depend on the CAC policy and what information it uses. But there is one important principle that applies regardless of the policy: if a CAC policy depends on a particular traffic parameter, then the network operator needs to ensure that the value the user has declared for that parameter is not exceeded during the actual flow of cells from the source. Only then can the network operator be confident that the performance requirements will be guaranteed. This is the job of usage parameter control.

9 Usage Parameter Control

"there's a hole in my bucket"

9.1 PROTECTING THE NETWORK

We have discussed the statistical multiplexing of traffic through ATM buffers and connection admission control mechanisms to limit the number of simultaneous connections, but how do we know that a traffic source is going to conform to the parameter values used in the admission control decision? There is nothing to stop a source sending cells over the access link at a far higher rate. It is the job of usage parameter control to ensure that any cells over and above the agreed values do not get any further into the network. These agreed values, including the performance requirements, are called the traffic contract.

Usage parameter control is defined as the set of actions taken by the network, at the user access, to monitor and control traffic in terms of conformity with the agreed traffic contract. The main purpose is to protect network resources from source traffic misbehaviour that could affect the quality of service of other established connections. UPC does this by detecting violations of negotiated parameters and taking appropriate actions, for example discarding or tagging cells, or clearing the connection.

A specific control algorithm has not been standardised. However any control algorithm should have the following desirable features:

- the ability to detect any traffic situation that does not conform to the traffic contract
- a rapid response to violations of the traffic contract, and
- it should be simple to implement.

But are all these features possible in one algorithm? Let's recall what parameters we want to check. The most important one is the peak cell rate; it is needed for both deterministic and statistical bit-rate transfer capabilities. For SBR, the traffic contract also contains the mean cell rate (for rate envelope multiplexing). With rate sharing statistical multiplexing, the burst length is additionally required. Before we look at a specific algorithm, let's consider the feasibility of controlling the mean cell rate.

9.2   CONTROLLING THE MEAN CELL RATE

Suppose we count the total number of cells being sent in some "measurement interval", T, by a Poisson source. The source has a declared mean cell rate, λ, of one cell per time unit. Is it correct to allow no more than one cell per time unit into the network? We know from Chapter 4 that the probability of k cells arriving in one time unit from a Poisson source is given by

$$\Pr\{k \text{ arrivals in one time unit}\} = \frac{(\lambda T)^k}{k!} e^{-\lambda T}$$

So the probability of more than one arrival per time unit is

$$= 1 - \frac{(1)^0}{0!} e^{-1} - \frac{(1)^1}{1!} e^{-1} = 0.2642$$

Thus this strict mean cell rate control would reject one or more cells from a well behaved Poisson source in 26 out of every 100 time units. What proportion of the number of cells does this represent? Well, we know that the mean number of cells per time unit is 1, and this can also be found by summing the probabilities of there being k cells weighted by the number of cells, k, i.e.

$$\text{mean number of cells} = 1 = 0\frac{(1)^0}{0!} e^{-1} + 1\frac{(1)^1}{1!} e^{-1} + 2\frac{(1)^2}{2!} e^{-1} + \cdots +$$
$$k\frac{(1)^k}{k!} e^{-1} + \cdots$$

When there are $k \geqslant 1$ cell arrivals in a time unit, then one cell is allowed on to the network and $k - 1$ are rejected. Thus the proportion of cells being allowed on to the network is

$$\frac{1\frac{(1)^1}{1!}e^{-1} + \sum_{k=2}^{\infty} 1\frac{(1)^k}{k!}e^{-1}}{1} = 0.6321$$

which means that almost 37% of cells are being rejected although the traffic contract is not being violated.

There are two options open to us: increase the maximum number of cells allowed into the network per time unit; or increase the measurement interval to many time units. The object is to decrease this proportion of cells being rejected to an acceptably low level, for example 1 in 10^{10}.

Let's define j as the maximum number of cells allowed into the network during time interval T. The first option requires us to find the smallest value of j for which the following inequality holds:

$$\frac{\sum_{k=j+1}^{\infty} \left\{ (k-j)\frac{(\lambda T)^k}{k!}e^{-\lambda T} \right\}}{\lambda T} \leqslant 10^{-10}$$

where, in this case, the mean cell rate of the source, λ, is 1 cell per time unit, and the measurement interval, T, is 1 time unit. Table 9.1 shows the proportion of cells rejected for a range of values of j.

To meet our requirement of no more than 1 in 10^{10} cells rejected for a Poisson source of mean rate 1 cell per time unit, we must accept up to 12 cells per time unit. If the Poisson source doubles its rate, then our limit of 12 cells per time unit would result in 1.2×10^{-7} of the cells being rejected. Ideally we would want 50% of the cells to be rejected to keep the source to its contracted mean of 1 cell per time unit. If the Poisson source increases its rate to 10 cells per time unit, then 5.3% of the cells are rejected, and hence over nine cells per time unit are allowed through. Thus measurement over a short interval means that either too many legitimate cells are rejected (if the limit is small) or, for cells which violate the contract, not enough are rejected (when the limit is large).

Let's now extend the measurement interval. Instead of tabulating for all values of j, the results are shown in Figure 9.1 for two different time intervals: 10 time units and 100 time units. For the 10^{-10} requirement, j is 37 (for $T = 10$) and 171 (for $T = 100$), i.e. the rate is limited to 3.7 cells per time unit, or 1.71 cells per time unit over the respective measurement intervals. So, as the measurement interval increases, the mean rate is being more closely controlled. The problem now is that the time taken to respond to violations of the contract is longer. This

Table 9.1
Proportion of cells rejected when no more than i cells are allowed per time unit

i	Proportion of cells rejected for a mean cell rate of		
	1 cell/time unit	2 cells/time unit	10 cells/time unit
1	3.68E-01	5.68E-01	9.00E-01
2	1.04E-01	2.71E-01	8.00E-01
3	2.33E-02	1.09E-01	7.00E-01
4	4.35E-03	3.76E-02	6.01E-01
5	6.89E-04	1.12E-02	5.04E-01
6	9.47E-05	2.96E-03	4.11E-01
7	1.15E-05	6.95E-04	3.24E-01
8	1.25E-06	1.47E-04	2.46E-01
9	1.22E-07	2.82E-05	1.79E-01
10	1.09E-08	4.96E-06	1.25E-01
11	9.00E-10	8.03E-07	8.34E-02
12	6.84E-11	1.21E-07	5.31E-02
13	4.84E-12	1.69E-08	3.22E-02
14	3.20E-13	2.21E-09	1.87E-02
15	1.98E-14	2.71E-10	1.03E-02

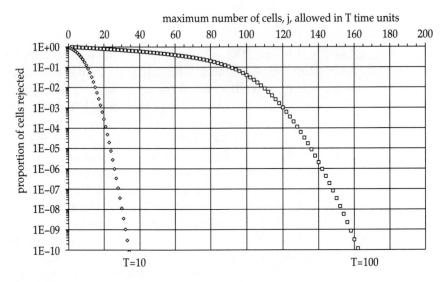

Figure 9.1
Proportion of cells rejected for limit of i cells in T time units

can result in action being taken too late to protect the network from the effect of the contract violation.

Figure 9.2 shows how the limit on the number of cells allowed per time unit varies with the measurement interval, for a rejection probability of 10^{-10}. The shorter the interval, the poorer the control of the

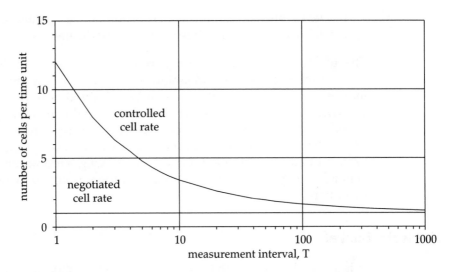

Figure 9.2
Controlling the mean cell rate over different timescales

mean rate because of the large "safety margin" required. The longer the interval, the slower the response to violations of the contract.

So we see that mean cell rate control requires a safety margin between the controlled cell rate and the negotiated cell rate to cope with the statistical fluctuations of well-behaved traffic streams, but this safety margin limits the ability of the UPC function to detect violations of the negotiated mean cell rate. As the measurement interval is extended, the safety margin required becomes less, but then any action in response to contract violation may be too late to be an effective protection for network resources.

Therefore we need to modify how we think of the mean cell rate: it is necessary to think in terms of a "virtual mean" defined over some specified time interval. The compromise is between the accuracy with which the cell rate is controlled, and the timeliness of any response to violations of the contract. Let's look at some algorithms which can monitor this virtual mean.

9.3   ALGORITHMS FOR UPC

Methods to control peak cell rate, mean cell rate and different load states within several timescales have been studied extensively. The most common algorithms involve two basic mechanisms:

- the window method, which limits the number of cells in a time window

• the leaky bucket method, which increments a counter for each cell arrival and decrements this counter periodically

The window method basically corresponds to the description given in the previous section and involves choosing a time interval and a maximum number of cells that can be admitted within that interval. We saw, with the Poisson source example, that the method suffers from either rejecting too many legitimate cells, or not rejecting enough when the contract is violated. A number of variations of the method have been studied (the jumping window, the moving window, and the exponentially weighted moving average), but there is not space to deal with them here.

The leaky bucket

It is generally agreed that the leaky bucket method achieves a better performance compromise than the window method. Leaky buckets are simple to understand and to implement, and flexible in application. Figure 9.3 illustrates the principle. Note that a separate control function is required for each virtual channel or virtual path being monitored.

A counter is incremented whenever a cell arrives; this counter, which is called the bucket, is also decremented at a constant "leak" rate. If the traffic source generates a burst of cells at a rate higher than the leak rate, the bucket begins to fill. Provided that the burst is short, the bucket will not fill up and no action will be taken against the cell stream. If a long enough burst of cells arrives at a rate higher than the leak rate, then the

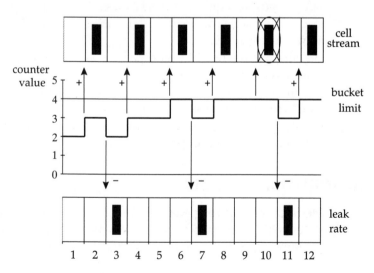

Figure 9.3
The operation of the leaky bucket

bucket will eventually overflow. In this case, each cell that arrives to find the counter at its maximum value is deemed to be in violation of the traffic contract and may be discarded, or "tagged" by changing the CLP bit in the cell header from high to low priority. Another possible course of action is for the connection to be released.

In Figure 9.3, the counter has a value of 2 at the start of the sequence. The leak rate is one every four cell slots and the traffic source being monitored is in a highly active state sending cells at a rate of 50% of the cell slot rate. It is not until the tenth cell slot in the sequence that a cell arrival finds the bucket on its limit. This non-conforming cell is then subject to discard or tagging. An important point to note is that the cells do not pass through the bucket, as though queueing in a buffer. Cells do not queue in the bucket, and therefore there is no variable delay through a leaky bucket. However, the operation of the bucket can be *analysed* as though it were a buffer with cells being served at the leak rate. This then allows us to find the probability that cells will be discarded or tagged by the UPC function.

9.4 PEAK CELL RATE CONTROL USING THE LEAKY BUCKET

If life was simple, then peak cell rate control would just involve a leaky bucket with a leak rate equal to the peak rate and a bucket depth of 1. The problem is the impact of cell-delay variation (CDV) which is introduced to the cell stream by the access network. Although a source may send cells with a constant inter-arrival time at the peak rate, those cells have to go through one or more buffers in the access network before they are monitored by the UPC algorithm on entry to the public network. The effect of queueing in those buffers is to vary the amount of delay experienced by each cell. Thus the time between successive cells from the same connection may be more than or less than the declared constant inter-arrival time.

For example, suppose there are five CBR sources, each with a peak rate of 10% of the cell slot rate, i.e. one cell every 10 slots, being multiplexed through an access switch with buffer capacity of 20 cells. If all the sources are out of phase, then none of the cells suffers any queueing delay in the access switch. However, if all the sources are in phase, then the worst delay will be for the last cell in the batch, i.e. a delay of four cell slots (the cell which is first to arrive enters service immediately and experiences no delay). Thus the maximum variation in delay is four cell slots. This worst case is illustrated in Figure 9.4. At the source, the inter-arrival times between cells 1 and 2, T_{12}, and cells 2 and 3, T_{23}, are both 10 cell slots. However, cell number 2 experiences the maximum CDV of four cell slots, and so on entry to the public network, the time between cells 2 and 3, T_{23} is reduced from 10 cell slots to six cell slots.

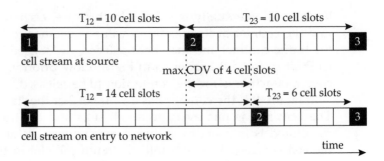

Figure 9.4
Effect of CDV in access network on inter-arrival times

This corresponds to a rate increase from 10% to 16.7% of the cell slot rate, i.e. a 67% increase on the declared peak cell rate.

It is obvious that the source itself is not to blame for this apparent increase in its peak cell rate; it is just a consequence of multiplexing in the access network. However, a strict peak cell rate control, with a leak rate of 10% of the cell slot rate and a bucket limit of 1, would penalise the connection by discarding cell number 3. How is this avoided? A CDV *tolerance* is needed for the UPC function, and this is achieved by increasing the leaky bucket limit.

Let's see how the leaky bucket would work in this situation. First, we must alter slightly our leaky bucket algorithm so that it can deal with any values of T (the inter-arrival time at the peak cell rate) and τ (the CDV tolerance). The leaky bucket counter works with integers, so we need to find integers k and n such that

$$\tau = k\frac{T}{n}$$

i.e. the inter-arrival time at the peak cell rate is divided into n equal parts, with n chosen so that the CDV tolerance is an integer multiple, k, of T/n. Then we operate the leaky bucket in the following way: the counter is incremented by n (the splash) when a cell arrives, and it is decremented at a leak rate of n/T. If the addition of a splash takes the counter above its limit of $k + n$, then the cell is in violation of the contract and is discarded or tagged. If the counter value is greater than n but less than or equal to $k + n$, then the cell is within the CDV tolerance and is allowed to enter the network.

Figure 9.5 shows how the counter value changes for the three cell arrivals of the example of Figure 9.4. In this case, $n = 10$, $k = 4$, the leak rate is equal to the cell slot rate, and the leaky bucket limit is $k + n = 14$. We assume that, when a cell arrives at the same time as the counter is decremented, the decrement takes place first followed

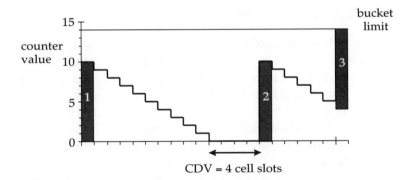

Figure 9.5
Example of cell stream with CDV within the tolerance

by the addition of the splash of n. Thus in the example shown, the counter reaches, but does not exceed, its limit at the arrival of cell number 3. This is because the inter-arrival time between cells 2 and 3 has suffered the maximum CDV permitted in the traffic contract which the leaky bucket is monitoring. Figure 9.6 shows what happens for the case when cell number 2 is delayed by five cell slots rather than four cell slots. The counter exceeds its limit when cell number 3 arrives, and so that cell must be discarded because it has violated the traffic contract.

The same principle applies if the tolerance, τ, exceeds the peak rate inter-arrival time, T, i.e. $k > n$. In this case it will take a number of successive cells with inter-arrival times less than T for the bucket to build up to its limit. Note that this extra parameter, the CDV tolerance, is an integral part of the traffic contract and must be specified in addition to the peak cell rate.

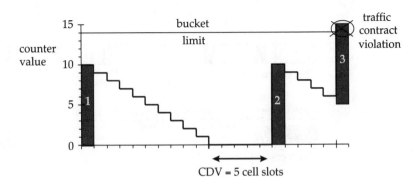

Figure 9.6
Example of cell stream with CDV exceeding the allowed tolerance

The problem of tolerances

When the CDV is greater than or equal to the inter-arrival time at the peak cell rate, the tolerance in the UPC function presents us with a problem. It is now possible to send multiple cells at the cell slot rate. The length of this burst is limited by the size of the bucket, but if the bucket is allowed to recover, i.e. the counter returns to zero, then another burst at the cell slot rate can be sent, and so on. Thus the consequence of introducing tolerances is to allow traffic with quite different characteristics to conform to the traffic contract.

An example of this worst case traffic is shown in Figure 9.7. The traffic contract is for a high bandwidth (one cell every five cell slots) CBR connection. With a CDV tolerance of 20 cell slots, we have $n = 1, k = 4$, the leak rate is the peak cell rate (20% of the cell slot rate), and the leaky bucket limit is $k + n = 5$. However, this allows a group of six cells to pass unhindered at the maximum cell rate of the link every 30 cell slots! So this worst case traffic is an on/off source of the same mean cell rate but at five times the peak cell rate.

How do we calculate this maximum burst size (MBS) at the cell slot rate, and the number of empty cell slots (ECS) between such bursts? We need to analyse the operation of the leaky bucket *as though it were* a queue with cells (sometimes called splashes) arriving and being served. The first n units in the leaky bucket effectively act as the service space for a splash. These n units are required for the leaky bucket to operate correctly on a peak cell rate whether or not there is any CDV tolerance. Thus it is in the extra k units where a queue forms, and so the leaky bucket limit of $k + n$ is equivalent to the *system capacity*.

So, we can analyse the formation of a queue by considering the time taken, t_{MBS}, for an excess rate to fill up the leaky bucket's *queueing space*, k:

$$t_{MBS} = \frac{\text{queueing space}}{\text{excess rate}} = \frac{k}{n\,\text{CSR} - n\,\text{PCR}}$$

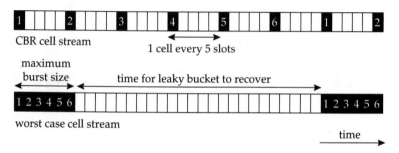

Figure 9.7
Worst case traffic for leaky bucket with CDV tolerance

where CSR is the cell slot rate, and PCR is the peak cell rate. We also know that

$$k = \tau \frac{n}{T} = \tau n \, \text{PCR}$$

so, substituting for k gives

$$t_{\text{MBS}} = \frac{\tau n \, \text{PCR}}{n(\text{CSR} - \text{PCR})} = \frac{\tau \text{PCR}}{\text{CSR} - \text{PCR}}$$

The maximum burst size is found by multiplying t_{MBS} by the cell slot rate and adding one for the first cell in the burst which fills the server space, n:

$$\text{MBS} = 1 + \lfloor \text{CSR} \, t_{\text{MBS}} \rfloor = 1 + \left\lfloor \frac{\tau \, \text{CSR} \, \text{PCR}}{\text{CSR} - \text{PCR}} \right\rfloor$$

which, in terms of the inter-arrival time at the peak rate, T, and the cell slot time, Δ, is

$$\text{MBS} = 1 + \left\lfloor \frac{\tau}{T - \Delta} \right\rfloor$$

We take the integer part of this calculation because there cannot be fractions of cells in a burst. For the example given in Figure 9.7, we have

$$\text{MBS} = 1 + \left\lfloor \frac{20}{5 - 1} \right\rfloor = 6 \text{ cells}$$

The time taken, t_{cycle}, for the leaky bucket to go through one complete cycle of filling, during the maximum burst, and then emptying, during the silence period is given by

$$n \, \text{MBS} = n \, \text{PCR} \, t_{\text{cycle}}$$

where the left hand side gives the total number of units by which the leaky bucket is incremented, and the right hand side gives the total number by which it is decremented. The total number of cell slots in a complete cycle is CSR t_{cycle}. It is necessary to round this up to the nearest integer number of cell slots to ensure that the leaky bucket empties completely, so the number of empty cell slots is

$$\text{ECS} = \left\lceil \text{CSR} \frac{\text{MBS}}{\text{PCR}} \right\rceil - \text{MBS}$$

For the example given in Figure 9.7, we have

$$\text{ECS} = \left\lceil 1\frac{6}{0.2} \right\rceil - 6 = 24 \text{ cells}$$

Resources required for a worst case ON/OFF cell stream from peak cell rate UPC

Continuing with this example, suppose that there are five of these CBR sources each being controlled by its own leaky bucket with the parameter values calculated. After the UPC function, the cell streams are multiplexed through an ATM buffer of capacity 20 cells. If the sources do in fact behave according to their declared contract, i.e. a peak cell rate of 20% of the cell slot rate, then there is no cell loss. In any five cell slots, we know that there will be exactly five cells arriving; this can be accommodated in the ATM buffer without loss.

But if all five sources behave as the worst case ON/OFF cell stream, then the situation is different. We know that in any 30 cell slots, there will be exactly 30 cells arriving. Whether the buffer capacity of 20 cells is sufficient depends on the relative phasing of the ON/OFF cell streams. If all five sources send a maximum burst at the same time, then 30 cells will arrive during six cell slots. This is an excess of 24 cells, 20 of which can be buffered, and four of which must be lost.

If we reduce the number of sources to four, their worst case behaviour will produce an aggregate burst of 24 cells arriving during six cell slots. This is an excess of 18 cells, all of which can be buffered. Thus the performance can be maintained only if the number of sources, and hence the admissible load, is reduced.

The example we have used is a very simple one which demonstrates the issue. A reduction from five sources admitted to four may not seem to be a severe consequence of CDV tolerances. In general, each CBR source of peak cell rate h cell/s is, in the worst case, being considered as an ON/OFF source with a *mean* cell rate of h cell/s and a peak cell rate equal to the cell slot rate of the link. This can reduce the admissible load by a significant amount.

We can estimate this load reduction by applying the $ND/D/1$ analysis to the worst case traffic streams. The application of this analysis rests on the observation that the worst case ON/OFF source is in fact periodic, with period MBS D. Each arrival is a burst of fixed size, MBS, which takes MBS cell slots to be served, so the period can be described as one burst in every D burst slots. A buffer of size X cells can hold $X/$MBS bursts, so we can adapt the analysis to deal with bursts rather than cells just by scaling the buffer capacity. The analysis does not account for the partial overlapping of bursts, but since we are only after an estimate we will neglect this detail.

The approximate analysis for the $ND/D/1$ queue tends to underestimate the loss, particularly when the load is not heavy. The effect of this is to overestimate the admissible load for a fixed CLP requirement. But the great advantage is that we can manipulate the formula to give the admissible load, ρ, as a function of the other parameters, X and D:

$$\rho = \frac{2(X+D)}{D\left(2 - \dfrac{\ln{(\mathrm{CLP})}}{X}\right)}$$

with the proviso that the load can never exceed a value of 1. This formula applies to the CBR cell streams. For the worst case streams, we just replace X by X/MBS to give:

$$\rho = \frac{2\left(\dfrac{X}{\mathrm{MBS}} + D\right)}{D\left(2 - \dfrac{\mathrm{MBS}\,\ln{(\mathrm{CLP})}}{X}\right)}$$

where

$$\mathrm{MBS} = 1 + \left\lfloor \frac{\tau}{T-\Delta} \right\rfloor = 1 + \left\lfloor \frac{\tau/\Delta}{D-1} \right\rfloor$$

Note that D is just the inter-arrival time, T, in units of the cell slot time, Δ.

Table 9.2 shows the number of sources ($N = \rho D$) that can be admitted for different CDV values and with a CLP requirement of 10^{-10}. It is assumed that the output cell streams from N UPC functions are multiplexed together over a 155.52 Mbit/s link (i.e. a cell slot rate of 353 208 cell/s). The link buffer has a capacity of 50 cells. The CDV tolerance allowed by the leaky buckets takes values of 20, 40, 60, 80 and 100 cell slots (corresponding to time values of 0.057, 0.113, 0.17, 0.226 and 0.283 ms respectively). The peak cell rates being monitored vary from 1% up to 10% of the cell slot rate. If the CDV tolerance is zero, then in this case the link can be loaded to 100% of capacity for each of the peak cell rates shown.

Figure 9.8 plots the data of Table 9.2 as the admissible load against the monitored peak cell rate. Note that when the CDV is relatively small (e.g. 40 cell slots or less), then there is little or no reduction in the admissible load in this example. The CDV in the access network may well be of this order, particularly if the access network utilisation is low and buffers are dimensioned to cope with only cell scale queueing and not burst scale queueing.

Table 9.2
Number of CBR sources that can be admitted over a 155.52 Mbit/s link with buffer capacity of 50 cells, for different CDV tolerances and a CLP of 10^{-10}

Period, D (slots)	Cell rate (cell/s)	$\tau/\Delta = 0$ slots $\tau = 0$ ms	Cell delay variation tolerance				
			20 slots 0.057 ms	40 slots 0.113 ms	60 slots 0.170 ms	80 slots 0.226 ms	100 slots 0.283 ms
10	35 321	10	10	9	6	5	3
11	32 110	11	11	9	6	5	4
12	29 434	12	12	12	8	6	5
13	27 170	13	13	13	8	7	6
14	25 229	14	14	13	11	8	7
15	23 547	15	15	15	11	9	7
16	22 075	16	16	16	12	10	8
17	20 777	17	17	17	15	10	9
18	19 623	18	18	18	15	13	11
19	18 590	19	19	19	16	13	11
20	17 660	20	20	20	16	13	11
21	16 819	21	21	21	17	14	12
22	16 055	22	22	22	22	17	14
23	15 357	23	23	23	23	18	15

24	14 717	24	24	24	24	19	15
25	14 128	25	25	25	24	19	16
26	13 585	26	26	26	25	20	16
27	13 082	27	27	27	25	20	20
28	12 615	28	28	28	26	26	21
29	12 180	29	29	29	27	27	21
30	11 774	30	30	30	27	27	21
35	10 092	35	35	35	35	30	30
40	8830	40	40	40	40	33	33
45	7849	45	45	45	45	45	36
50	7064	50	50	50	50	50	39
55	6422	55	55	55	54	54	54
60	5887	60	60	60	58	58	58
65	5434	65	65	65	65	61	61
70	5046	70	70	70	70	65	65
75	4709	75	75	75	75	68	68
80	4415	80	80	80	80	71	71
85	4155	85	85	85	85	85	75
90	3925	90	90	90	90	90	78
95	3718	95	95	95	95	95	82
100	3532	100	100	100	100	100	85

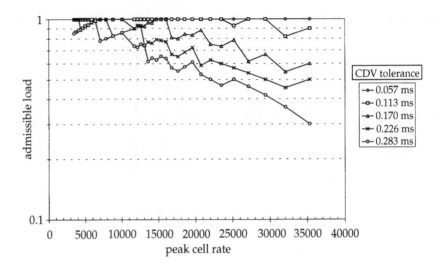

Figure 9.8
Admissible load for CBR sources with different CDV tolerances

Traffic shaping

One solution to the problem of worst case traffic is to introduce a spacer after the leaky bucket in order to enforce a minimum time between cells, corresponding to the particular peak cell-rate being monitored by the leaky bucket. Spacing is performed only on those cells which conform to the traffic contract; this prevents the "bunching together" of cells (whether of the worst case traffic, or caused by variation in cell delay within the CDV tolerance of the traffic contract). However, spacing introduces extra complexity which is required on a per connection basis. The leaky bucket is just a simple counter — a spacer requires buffer storage and introduces delay.

9.5   DUAL LEAKY BUCKETS: THE LEAKY CUP AND SAUCER

Consider the situation for a variable rate source described by a peak cell rate and a mean cell rate. This can be monitored by two leaky buckets: one to control the peak cell rate, the other to control a "virtual mean" cell rate. In ITU Recommendation I.371 the term used for this "virtual mean" is the sustainable cell rate (SCR). With two leaky buckets, the effect of the CDV tolerance on the peak cell rate leaky bucket is not so severe. The reason is that the leaky bucket for the sustainable cell rate limits the number of worst case bursts that can pass through the peak cell rate leaky bucket. For each ON/OFF cycle at the cell slot rate, the SCR leaky bucket increases by a certain amount. When the SCR leaky bucket reaches its limit, the ON/OFF cycles must stop until the SCR counter has returned to zero. So the maximum burst size is still determined by the PCR leaky bucket parameter values, but the overall mean cell rate allowed onto the network is limited by the sustainable cell rate rather than the peak cell rate.

This dual leaky bucket arrangement is called the leaky "cup and saucer". The cup is the leaky bucket for the sustainable cell rate: it is a deep container with a base of relatively small diameter. The saucer is the leaky bucket for the peak cell rate: it is a shallow container with a large diameter base. The depth corresponds to the bucket limit and the diameter of the base to the cell rate being controlled.

The worst case traffic is shown in Figure 9.9(a). The effect of the leaky buckets is to limit the number of cells over different time periods. For the example in the figure, the saucer limit is two cells in four cell slots and the cup limit is six cells in 24 cell slots. An alternative "worst case" traffic which is adopted in ITU draft Recommendation E.73x is an ON/OFF source with maximum length bursts at the peak cell rate rather than at the cell slot rate. An example of this type of worst case traffic is shown in Figure 9.9(b). Note that the time axis is in cell slots, so the area under the curve is equal to the number of cells sent.

The maximum burst size at the peak cell rate is obtained in a similar way to that at the cell slot rate, i.e.

$$MBS = 1 + \left\lfloor \frac{\tau_{IBT}}{T_{SCR} - T_{PCR}} \right\rfloor$$

where τ_{IBT} is called the intrinsic burst tolerance. This is another important parameter in the traffic contract (in addition to the inter-arrival times T_{SCR} and T_{PCR} for the sustainable and peak cell rates respectively). The purpose of the intrinsic burst tolerance is in fact to specify the burst length limit in the traffic contract.

Two CDV tolerances are specified in the traffic contract. We are already familiar with the CDV tolerance, τ, for the peak cell rate. From now on we call this τ_{PCR} to distinguish it from the CDV tolerance for the sustainable cell rate, τ'_{SCR}. This latter has to be added to the intrinsic burst tolerance in order to determine the counter limit for the cup. As before, we need to find integers, k and n such that

$$\tau_{IBT} + \tau'_{SCR} = k \frac{T_{SCR}}{n}$$

In most cases, n can be set to one because the intrinsic burst tolerance will be many times larger than T_{SCR}.

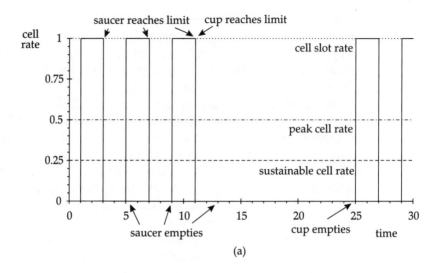

(a)

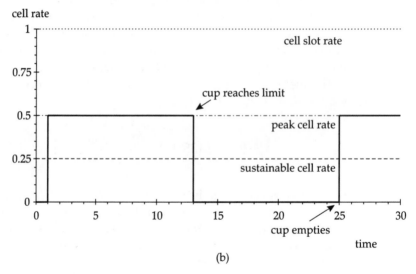

(b)

Figure 9.9
Worst case traffic through leaky cup and saucer

Resources required for a worst case ON/OFF cell stream from sustainable cell rate UPC

Both types of "worst case" traffic shown in Figure 9.9 are not easy to analyse. In the following analysis we use the maximum burst size for the sustainable cell rate, and assume that that burst actually arrives at the cell slot rate. Whether or not this is possible depends on the size of the saucer, and hence on τ_{PCR}. It is likely to be the worst of all possible traffic streams because it generates the largest burst size.

The same approximate analytical approach is taken as before. In this case D is the inter-arrival time, T_{SCR}, in units of the cell slot time, Δ.

$$\rho = \frac{2\left(\dfrac{X}{\text{MBS}} + D\right)}{D\left(2 - \dfrac{\text{MBS } \ln(\text{CLP})}{X}\right)}.$$

A graph of utilisation against the maximum burst size is shown in Figure 9.10. The CLP requirement varies from 10^{-4} down to 10^{-10}. The link buffer has a capacity of 50 cells, the cell slot rate is 353 208 cell/s, and the sustainable cell rate is chosen to be 3532 cell/s, i.e. $D = 100$. The maximum burst size allowed by the leaky cup and saucer is varied from one up to 50 cells. The peak cell rate and intrinsic burst tolerance are not specified explicitly; different combinations can be calculated from the maximum burst size and the sustainable cell rate.

It is important to use the correct value of MBS because this obviously can have a significant effect on the admissible load. Suppose that the peak cell rate is twice the sustainable cell rate, i.e. $T_{PCR} = T_{SCR}/2$. The maximum burst size at the peak cell rate is

$$\text{MBS}_{PCR} = 1 + \left\lfloor \frac{\tau_{IBT}}{T_{SCR} - \dfrac{T_{SCR}}{2}} \right\rfloor = 1 + \left\lfloor \frac{2\tau_{IBT}}{T_{SCR}} \right\rfloor$$

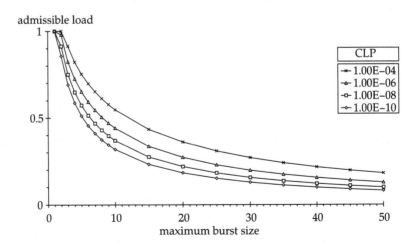

Figure 9.10
Admissible load for worst case traffic through leaky cup and saucer

and the maximum burst size at the cell slot rate is

$$\mathrm{MBS_{CSR}} = 1 + \left\lfloor \frac{\tau_{\mathrm{IBT}}}{T_{\mathrm{SCR}} - \Delta} \right\rfloor \approx 1 + \left\lfloor \frac{\tau_{\mathrm{IBT}}}{T_{\mathrm{SCR}}} \right\rfloor$$

The difference between these two maximum size bursts is almost a factor of two (for reasonable values of the intrinsic burst tolerance), and this corresponds to a difference in the admissible load of a factor of roughly 0.6 across the range of burst sizes in the graph. So the assumption that the worst case traffic is based on the maximum burst size at the peak cell rate carries with it a 40% penalty on the admissible load.

10 Dimensioning

real networks don't lose cells?

10.1 COMBINING THE BURST AND CELL SCALES

The finite capacity buffer is a fundamental element of ATM where cells multiplexed from a number of different input streams are temporarily stored awaiting onward transmission. The flow of cells from the different inputs, the number of inputs, and the rate at which cells are served determine the occupancy of the buffer and hence the cell delay and cell loss experienced. So, how large should this finite buffer be?

In Chapters 6 and 7 we have seen that there are two elements of queueing behaviour: the cell scale and burst scale components. We evaluated the loss from a finite buffer for constant bit-rate, variable bit-rate and random traffic sources. For random traffic, or for a mix of CBR traffic, only the cell scale component is present. But when the traffic mix includes bursty sources, such that combinations of the active states can exceed the cell slot rate, then both components of queueing are present.

Let's look at each type of traffic and see how the loss varies with the buffer size for different offered loads. We can then develop strategies for buffer dimensioning based on an understanding of this behaviour. Firstly, we consider VBR traffic; this combines the cell scale component of queueing with both the loss and delay factors of the burst scale component of queueing.

Figure 7.14 shows how the burst scale loss factor varies with the number of sources, N, where each source has a peak cell rate of 24 000 cell/s and a mean cell rate of 2000 cell/s. From Table 7.2 we find that the minimum number of these sources required for burst scale queueing is $N_0 = 14.72$. Table 10.1 gives the burst scale loss factor, CLP_{bsl}, at three different values of N (30, 60 and 90 sources) as well as the offered load as a fraction of the cell slot rate (calculated using the bufferless analysis in Chapter 7). These values of load are used to calculate both the cell scale queueing component, CLP_{cs}, and the burst scale delay factor, CLP_{bsd}, varying with buffer capacity.

The combined results are plotted in Figure 10.1. The cell scale component is obtained using the exact analysis of the finite $M/D/1$ described in Chapter 5. The burst scale delay factor uses the same approach as that for calculating the values in Figure 7.16. For Figure 10.1, an average burst length, b, of 480 cells is used. The overall cell loss shown in Figure 10.1 is calculated by summing the burst and cell scale components of cell loss, where the burst scale component is the product of the loss and delay factors, i.e.

$$CLP = CLP_{cs} + CLP_{bsl}CLP_{bsd}$$

Table 10.1
Burst scale loss factor for
N VBR sources

N	CLP_{bsl}	load
30	4.46E-10	0.17
60	1.11E-05	0.34
90	9.10E-04	0.51

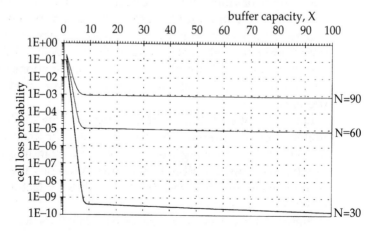

Figure 10.1
Overall cell loss probability against buffer capacity for N VBR sources

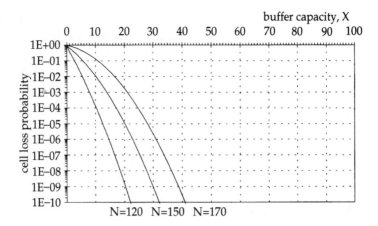

Figure 10.2
Cell loss probability against buffer capacity for N CBR sources

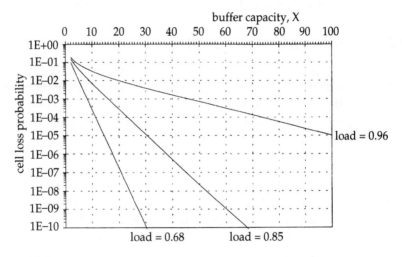

Figure 10.3
Cell loss probability against buffer capacity for random traffic

Now, consider N CBR sources where each source has a constant cell rate of 2000 cell/s. Figure 10.2 shows how the cell loss varies with the buffer capacity for 120, 150 and 170 sources. The corresponding values for the offered load are 0.68, 0.85, and 0.96 respectively. Figure 10.3 takes the load values used for the CBR traffic and assumes that the traffic is random. The cell loss results are found using the exact analysis for the finite $M/D/1$ system. A summary of the three different situations is depicted in Figure 10.4, comparing 30 VBR sources, 150 CBR sources, and an offered load of 0.85 of random traffic (the same load as 150 CBR sources).

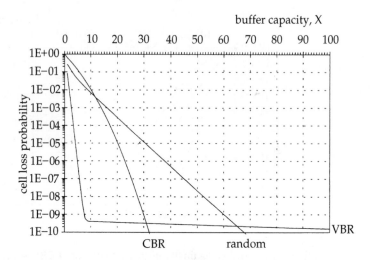

Figure 10.4
Comparison of VBR, CBR and random traffic through a finite buffer

10.2   DIMENSIONING THE BUFFER

Figure 10.4 shows three very different curves, depending on the characteristics of each different type of source. There is no question that the buffer must be able to cope with the cell scale component of queueing since this is always present when a number of traffic streams are merged. But we have two options when it comes to the burst scale component, as analysed in Chapter 7:

1.   Restrict the number of bursty sources so that the total input rate only rarely exceeds the cell slot rate, and assume that all excess-rate cells are lost. This is the bufferless or burst scale loss option (also known as rate envelope multiplexing).

2.   Assume that we have a big enough buffer to cope with excess-rate cells, so only a proportion are lost; the other excess-rate cells are delayed in the buffer. This is the burst scale delay option (rate sharing statistical multiplexing).

It is important to notice that how big we make the buffer, depends on how we intend to accept traffic onto the network (or vice versa). Also a dimensioning choice has an impact on a control mechanism (connection admission control).

   For the first option, the buffer is dimensioned according to cell scale constraints. The amount of bursty traffic is not the limiting factor in choosing the buffer capacity because the CAC restrictions on accepting bursty traffic automatically limit the burst scale component to a value

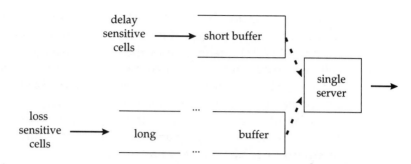

a time priority scheme would involve serving cells
in the short buffer before cells in the long buffer

Figure 10.5
Time priorities and segregation of traffic

below the CLP requirement, and the CAC algorithm assumes that the buffer size makes no difference. Thus for bursty traffic the mean utilisation is low and the gradient of its cell scale component is steep (see Figure 10.1). However, for either constant bit-rate or random traffic, the cell scale component is much more significant (there is no burst scale component), and it is a realistic maximum load of this traffic that determines the buffer capacity. The limiting factor here is the delay through the buffer, particularly for interactive services.

If we choose the second option, the amount of bursty traffic can be increased to the same levels of utilisation as for either constant bit-rate or random traffic — the price to pay is in the size of the buffer which must be significantly larger. The disadvantage with buffering the excess (burst scale) cells is that the delay through a *large* buffer can be too great for services like telephony and interactive video, which negates the aims of having an integrated approach to all telecommunications services. There are ways around the problem — segregation of traffic through separate buffers and the use of time priority servers — but this does introduce further complexity into the network, see Figure 10.5. We will look at these in more detail in Chapter 11.

Small buffers for cell scale queueing

A comparison of random traffic and CBR traffic (see Figure 10.4) shows that the "cell scale component" of the random traffic gives a worse CLP for the same load. Even with 1000 CBR sources, each of 300 cell/s (to keep the load constant at 0.85), Table 8.3(b) shows that the cell loss is about 10^{-9} for a buffer capacity of 50 cells. This is a factor of 10 lower than for random traffic through the same size buffer.

So, to dimension buffers for cell scale queueing we use a realistic maximum load of *random* traffic. Table 10.2 uses the exact analysis for the finite $M/D/1$ queue to show the buffer capacity for a given load and cell loss probability. The first column is the load, varying from 50% up to 98%, and the second column gives the buffer size for a particular cell loss probability requirement (Table 10.2 part (a) is for a CLP of 10^{-8}, part (b) is for 10^{-10}, and part (c) is for 10^{-12}). Then there are extra columns which give the mean delay and maximum delay through the buffer for link rates of 155.52 Mbit/s and 622.08 Mbit/s. The maximum delay is just the buffer capacity multiplied by the time per cell slot, s, at the appropriate link rate. The mean delay depends on the load, ρ, and is calculated using the formula for an infinite M/D/1 system:

$$t_q = s + \frac{\rho s}{2(1 - \rho)}$$

This is very close to the mean delay through a finite M/D/1 because the loss is extremely low (mean delays only differ noticeably when the loss from the finite system is high).

Figure 10.6 presents the mean and maximum delay values from Table 10.2 in the form of a graph and clearly shows how the delays increase substantially above a load of about 80%. This graph can be used to select a maximum load according to the cell loss and delay constraints, and the buffer's link rate; the required buffer size can then be read from the appropriate part of Table 10.2.

So, to summarise, we dimension short buffers to cope with cell scale queueing behaviour using Table 10.2 and Figure 10.6. This approach is applicable to networks which offer the deterministic bit-rate transfer capability and the statistical bit-rate transfer capability based on rate envelope multiplexing. For SBR based on rate sharing, buffer dimensioning requires a different approach, based on the burst scale queueing behaviour.

Large buffers for burst scale queueing

A buffer dimensioning method for large buffers and burst scale queueing is rather more complicated than for short buffers and cell scale queueing because the traffic characterisation has more parameters. For the cell scale queueing case, random traffic is a very good upper bound and it has just the one parameter: arrival rate. In the burst scale queueing case, we must assume a traffic mix of many on/off sources, each source having the same traffic characteristics (peak cell rate, mean cell rate, and the mean burst length in the active state). For the burst scale analytical approach we described in Chapter 7, the key parameters are

Table 10.2(a)
Buffer dimensioning for cell scale queueing: buffer capacity, mean and maximum delay, given the offered load and a cell loss probability of 10^{-8}

Load	Buffer capacity (cells)	155.52 Mbit/s link		622.08 Mbit/s link	
		mean delay (μs)	maximum delay (μs)	mean delay (μs)	maximum delay (μs)
0.50	16	4.2	45.3	1.1	11.3
0.51	16	4.3	45.3	1.1	11.3
0.52	17	4.4	48.1	1.1	12.0
0.53	17	4.4	48.1	1.1	12.0
0.54	17	4.5	48.1	1.1	12.0
0.55	18	4.6	51.0	1.1	12.7
0.56	18	4.6	51.0	1.2	12.7
0.57	19	4.7	53.8	1.2	13.4
0.58	19	4.8	53.8	1.2	13.4
0.59	20	4.9	56.6	1.2	14.2
0.60	20	5.0	56.6	1.2	14.2
0.61	21	5.0	59.5	1.3	14.9
0.62	21	5.1	59.5	1.3	14.9
0.63	22	5.2	62.3	1.3	15.6
0.64	23	5.3	65.1	1.3	16.3
0.65	23	5.5	65.1	1.4	16.3
0.66	24	5.6	67.9	1.4	17.0
0.67	25	5.7	70.8	1.4	17.7
0.68	25	5.8	70.8	1.5	17.7
0.69	26	6.0	73.6	1.5	18.4
0.70	27	6.1	76.4	1.5	19.1
0.71	28	6.3	79.3	1.6	19.8
0.72	29	6.5	82.1	1.6	20.5
0.73	30	6.7	84.9	1.7	21.2
0.74	31	6.9	87.8	1.7	21.9
0.75	33	7.1	93.4	1.8	23.4
0.76	34	7.3	96.3	1.8	24.1
0.77	35	7.6	99.1	1.9	24.8
0.78	37	7.9	104.8	2.0	26.2
0.79	39	8.2	110.4	2.0	27.6
0.80	41	8.5	116.1	2.1	29.0
0.81	43	8.9	121.7	2.2	30.4
0.82	45	9.3	127.4	2.3	31.9
0.83	48	9.7	135.9	2.4	34.0
0.84	51	10.3	144.4	2.6	36.1
0.85	54	10.9	152.9	2.7	38.2
0.86	58	11.5	164.2	2.9	41.1
0.87	62	12.3	175.5	3.1	43.9
0.88	67	13.2	189.7	3.3	47.4
0.89	73	14.3	206.7	3.6	51.7
0.90	79	15.6	223.7	3.9	55.9
0.91	88	17.1	249.1	4.3	62.3
0.92	98	19.1	277.5	4.8	69.4
0.93	112	21.6	317.1	5.4	79.3
0.94	129	25.0	365.2	6.3	91.3
0.95	153	29.7	433.2	7.4	108.3
0.96	189	36.8	535.1	9.2	133.8
0.97	248	48.6	702.1	12.2	175.5
0.98	362	72.2	1024.9	18.0	256.2

Table 10.2(b)
Buffer dimensioning for cell scale queueing: buffer capacity, mean and maximum delay, given the offered load and a cell loss probability of 10^{-10}

Load	Buffer capacity (cells)	155.52 Mbit/s link		622.08 Mbit/s link	
		mean delay (μs)	maximum delay (μs)	mean delay (μs)	maximum delay (μs)
0.50	19	4.2	53.8	1.1	13.4
0.51	20	4.3	56.6	1.1	14.2
0.52	20	4.4	56.6	1.1	14.2
0.53	21	4.4	59.5	1.1	14.9
0.54	21	4.5	59.5	1.1	14.9
0.55	22	4.6	62.3	1.1	15.6
0.56	23	4.6	65.1	1.2	16.3
0.57	23	4.7	65.1	1.2	16.3
0.58	24	4.8	67.9	1.2	17.0
0.59	24	4.9	67.9	1.2	17.0
0.60	25	5.0	70.8	1.2	17.7
0.61	26	5.0	73.6	1.3	18.4
0.62	26	5.1	73.6	1.3	18.4
0.63	27	5.2	76.4	1.3	19.1
0.64	28	5.3	79.3	1.3	19.8
0.65	29	5.5	82.1	1.4	20.5
0.66	30	5.6	84.9	1.4	21.2
0.67	31	5.7	87.8	1.4	21.9
0.68	32	5.8	90.6	1.5	22.6
0.69	33	6.0	93.4	1.5	23.4
0.70	34	6.1	96.3	1.5	24.1
0.71	35	6.3	99.1	1.6	24.8
0.72	37	6.5	104.8	1.6	26.2
0.73	38	6.7	107.6	1.7	26.9
0.74	39	6.9	110.4	1.7	27.6
0.75	41	7.1	116.1	1.8	29.0
0.76	43	7.3	121.7	1.8	30.4
0.77	45	7.6	127.4	1.9	31.9
0.78	47	7.9	133.1	2.0	33.3
0.79	49	8.2	138.7	2.0	34.7
0.80	51	8.5	144.4	2.1	36.1
0.81	54	8.9	152.9	2.2	38.2
0.82	57	9.3	161.4	2.3	40.3
0.83	60	9.7	169.9	2.4	42.5
0.84	64	10.3	181.2	2.6	45.3
0.85	68	10.9	192.5	2.7	48.1
0.86	73	11.5	206.7	2.9	51.7
0.87	79	12.3	223.7	3.1	55.9
0.88	85	13.2	240.7	3.3	60.2
0.89	93	14.3	263.3	3.6	65.8
0.90	102	15.6	288.8	3.9	72.2
0.91	113	17.1	319.9	4.3	80.0
0.92	126	19.1	356.7	4.8	89.2
0.93	144	21.6	407.7	5.4	101.9
0.94	167	25.0	472.8	6.3	118.2
0.95	199	29.7	563.4	7.4	140.9
0.96	246	36.8	696.5	9.2	174.1
0.97	324	48.6	917.3	12.2	229.3
0.98	476	72.2	1347.6	18.0	336.9

Table 10.2(c)

Buffer dimensioning for cell scale queueing: buffer capacity, mean and maximum delay, given the offered load and a cell loss probability of 10^{-12}

Load	Buffer capacity (cells)	155.52 Mbit/s link		622.08 Mbit/s link	
		mean delay (μs)	maximum delay (μs)	mean delay (μs)	maximum delay (μs)
0.50	23	4.2	65.1	1.1	16.3
0.51	24	4.3	67.9	1.1	17.0
0.52	24	4.4	67.9	1.1	17.0
0.53	25	4.4	70.8	1.1	17.7
0.54	26	4.5	73.6	1.1	18.4
0.55	26	4.6	73.6	1.1	18.4
0.56	27	4.6	76.4	1.2	19.1
0.57	28	4.7	79.3	1.2	19.8
0.58	28	4.8	79.3	1.2	19.8
0.59	29	4.9	82.1	1.2	20.5
0.60	30	5.0	84.9	1.2	21.2
0.61	31	5.0	87.8	1.3	21.9
0.62	32	5.1	90.6	1.3	22.6
0.63	33	5.2	93.4	1.3	23.4
0.64	34	5.3	96.3	1.3	24.1
0.65	35	5.5	99.1	1.4	24.8
0.66	36	5.6	101.9	1.4	25.5
0.67	37	5.7	104.8	1.4	26.2
0.68	38	5.8	107.6	1.5	26.9
0.69	39	6.0	110.4	1.5	27.6
0.70	41	6.1	116.1	1.5	29.0
0.71	42	6.3	118.9	1.6	29.7
0.72	44	6.5	124.6	1.6	31.1
0.73	46	6.7	130.2	1.7	32.6
0.74	47	6.9	133.1	1.7	33.3
0.75	49	7.1	138.7	1.8	34.7
0.76	52	7.3	147.2	1.8	36.8
0.77	54	7.6	152.9	1.9	38.2
0.78	56	7.9	158.5	2.0	39.6
0.79	59	8.2	167.0	2.0	41.8
0.80	62	8.5	175.5	2.1	43.9
0.81	65	8.9	184.0	2.2	46.0
0.82	69	9.3	195.4	2.3	48.8
0.83	73	9.7	206.7	2.4	51.7
0.84	78	10.3	220.8	2.6	55.2
0.85	83	10.9	235.0	2.7	58.7
0.86	89	11.5	252.0	2.9	63.0
0.87	96	12.3	271.8	3.1	67.9
0.88	104	13.2	294.4	3.3	73.6
0.89	113	14.3	319.9	3.6	80.0
0.90	124	15.6	351.1	3.9	87.8
0.91	138	17.1	390.7	4.3	97.7
0.92	154	19.1	436.0	4.8	109.0
0.93	176	21.6	498.3	5.4	124.6
0.94	204	25.0	577.6	6.3	144.4
0.95	244	29.7	690.8	7.4	172.7
0.96	303	36.8	857.9	9.2	214.5
0.97	400	48.6	1132.5	12.2	283.1
0.98	592	72.2	1676.1	18.0	419.0

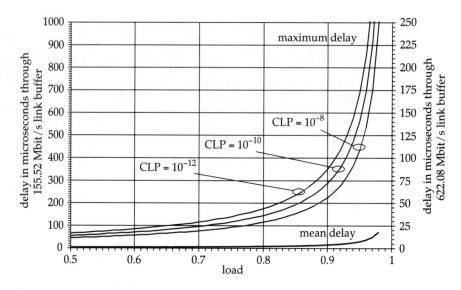

Figure 10.6
Mean and maximum delays for a buffer with link rate of either 155.52 Mbit/s or 622.08 Mbit/s for cell loss probabilities of 10^{-8}, 10^{-10}, and 10^{-12}

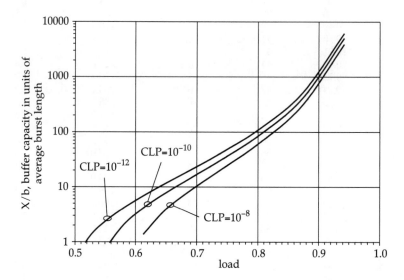

Figure 10.7
Buffer capacity in units of mean burst length, given load and cell loss probability, for traffic with a peak cell rate of 1/100 of the cell slot rate (i.e. $N_0 = 100$)

the minimum number of peak rates required for burst scale queueing, N_0, the ratio of buffer capacity to mean burst length, X/b, the mean load, ρ, and the cell loss probability.

We have seen in Chapter 8 that the overall cell loss target can be obtained by trial and error with tables; combining the burst scale loss

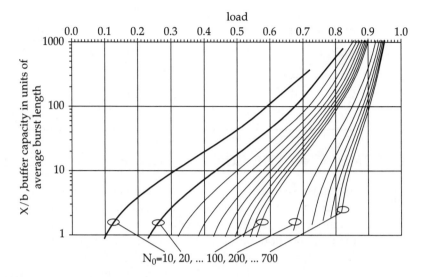

Figure 10.8
Buffer capacity in units of mean burst length, given load and the ratio of cell slot rate to peak cell rate, for a cell loss probability of 10^{-10}

and burst scale delay factors from Table 8.4 and Table 8.5 respectively. Here, we present buffer dimensioning data in two alternative graphical forms: the variation of X/b with load for a fixed value of N_0 and different overall CLP values (Figure 10.7); and the variation of X/b with load for a fixed overall CLP value and different values of N_0 (Figure 10.8).

To produce a graph like that of Figure 10.7, we take one row from Table 8.4, for a particular value of N_0. This gives the cell loss contribution, CLP_{bsl}, from the burst scale loss factor varying with offered load (Table 10.3). We then need to find the value of X/b which gives a cell loss contribution, CLP_{bsd}, from the burst scale delay factor, to meet the overall CLP target. This is found by rearranging the equation:

$$\frac{\text{CLP}_{target}}{\text{CLP}_{bsl}} = \text{CLP}_{bsd} = \exp\left[-N_0 \frac{X}{b} \frac{(1-\rho)^3}{4\rho+1}\right]$$

to give

$$\frac{X}{b} = -\frac{4\rho+1}{(1-\rho)^3} \frac{\ln\left(\text{CLP}_{target}/\text{CLP}_{bsl}\right)}{N_0}$$

Table 10.3 gives the figures for an overall CLP target of 10^{-10}, and Figure 10.7 shows results for three different CLP targets: 10^{-8}, 10^{-10} and 10^{-12}. Figure 10.8 shows results for a range of values of N_0 for an overall CLP target of 10^{-10}.

Table 10.3
Burst scale parameter values for $N_0 = 100$ and a CLP target of 10^{-10}

CLP$_{bsd}$	10^{-1}	10^{-2}	10^{-3}	10^{-4}	10^{-5}	10^{-6}	10^{-7}	10^{-8}	10^{-9}	10^{-10}
load, ρ	0.94	0.87	0.80	0.74	0.69	0.65	0.61	0.58	0.55	0.53
CLP$_{bsd}$	10^{-9}	10^{-8}	10^{-7}	10^{-6}	10^{-5}	10^{-4}	10^{-3}	10^{-2}	10^{-1}	10^{-0}
X/b	5064.2	394.2	84.6	31.1	14.7	7.7	4.1	2.1	0.8	0

10.3 COMBINING THE CONNECTION, BURST AND CELL SCALES

We have seen in Chapter 8 that connection admission control can be based on a variety of different algorithms. An important grade of service parameter, in addition to cell loss and cell delay, is the probability of a connection being blocked. This is very much dependent on the CAC algorithm and the characteristics of the offered traffic types, and in general it is a difficult task to evaluate the connection blocking probability.

However, if we restrict the CAC algorithm to one that is based on limiting the *number* of connections admitted, then we can apply Erlang's lost call formula to the situation. The service capacity of an ATM link is effectively being divided into N "circuits". If all of these "circuits" are occupied, then the CAC algorithm will reject any further connection attempts. It is worth noting that the cell loss and cell delay performance requirements determine the *maximum* number of connections that can be admitted. Thus for much of the time, the traffic mix will have fewer connections, and the cell loss and cell delay performance will be rather better than that specified in the traffic contract requirements.

Consider the situation with constant bit-rate traffic. Figure 10.9 plots the cell loss from a buffer of capacity 10 cells, for a range of CBR sources where D is the number of slots between arrivals. Thus, with a particular CLP requirement, and a constant cell rate given by

$$h = \frac{C}{D} \text{ cell/s}$$

(where C is the cell slot rate), we can find from Figure 10.9 the maximum number of connections that can be admitted onto a link of cell rate C. The link cannot be loaded to more than 100% capacity, so the maximum possible number of sources of any particular type is numerically equal to the (constant) number of cell slots between arrivals. Let's take an example. Suppose we have CBR sources of cell rate 3532 cell/s being multiplexed over a 155.52 Mbit/s link, with a CLP requirement of 10^{-7}. This gives a value of 100 for D, and from Figure 10.9, the maximum number of connections is (near enough) 50.

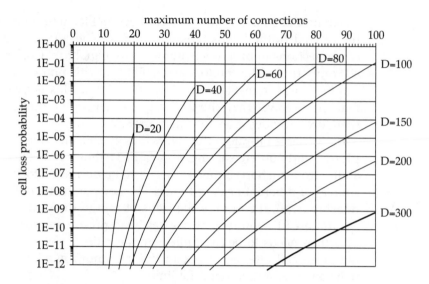

Figure 10.9
Maximum number of CBR connections, given D cell slots between arrivals and CLP

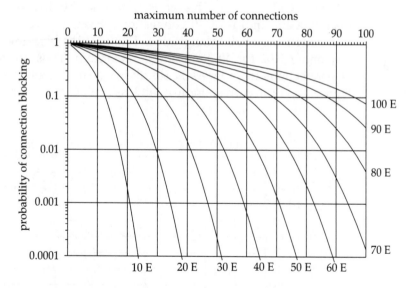

Figure 10.10
Probability of blocking, given maximum number of connections and offered traffic

Now that we have a figure for the maximum number of connections, we can calculate the offered traffic at the connection level for a given probability of blocking. Figure 10.10 shows how the connection blocking probability varies with the maximum number of connections for different offered traffic intensities. With our example, we find that for

50 connections maximum and a connection blocking probability of 0.02, the offered traffic intensity is 40 Erlangs. Note that the mean number of connections in progress is numerically equal to the offered traffic, i.e. 40 connections. The cell loss probability for this number of connections can be found from Figure 10.9: it is 2×10^{-9}. This is over an order of magnitude lower than the CLP requirement in the traffic contract, and therefore provides a useful safety margin.

For variable bit-rate traffic, we will only consider rate envelope multiplexing and not rate sharing. Figure 10.11 shows how the cell loss probability from a (short) buffer varies with the utilisation for a range of VBR sources of different peak cell rates. The key parameter defining this relationship is N_0, the ratio of the cell slot rate to the peak cell rate. Given N_0 and a CLP requirement, we can read off a value for the utilisation. This then needs to be multiplied by the ratio of the cell slot rate, C, to the mean cell rate, m, to obtain the maximum number of connections that can be admitted onto the link.

So, for example, for sources with a peak cell rate of 8830 cell/s and a mean cell rate of 3532 cell/s being multiplexed onto a 155.52 Mbit/s link, N_0 is 40 and, according to Figure 10.11, the utilisation is about 0.4 for a CLP of 10^{-8}. This utilisation is multiplied by 100 (i.e. C/m) to give a maximum of 40 connections. From Figure 10.10, an offered traffic intensity of 30 Erlangs gives a connection blocking probability of just under 0.02 for 40 connections maximum. Thus the mean number of connections in progress is 30, giving a mean load of 0.3, and from Figure 10.11 the corresponding cell loss probability is found to be 10^{-11}.

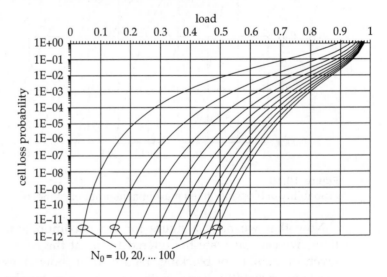

Figure 10.11
Maximum utilisation for VBR connections, given N_0 and CLP

Table 10.4
Traffic table based on Erlang's lost call formula

N	Probability of blocking a connection						
	0.1	0.05	0.02	0.01	0.005	0.001	0.0001
	Offered traffic in Erlangs:						
1	0.11	0.05	0.02	0.01	0.005	0.001	0.0001
2	0.59	0.38	0.22	0.15	0.10	0.04	0.03
3	1.27	0.89	0.60	0.45	0.34	0.19	0.08
4	2.04	1.52	1.09	0.86	0.70	0.43	0.23
5	2.88	2.21	1.65	1.36	1.13	0.76	0.45
6	3.75	2.96	2.27	1.90	1.62	1.14	0.72
7	4.66	3.73	2.93	2.50	2.15	1.57	1.05
8	5.59	4.54	3.62	3.12	2.72	2.05	1.42
9	6.54	5.37	4.34	3.78	3.33	2.55	1.82
10	7.51	6.21	5.08	4.46	3.96	3.09	2.26
11	8.48	7.07	5.84	5.15	4.61	3.65	2.72
12	9.47	7.95	6.61	5.87	5.27	4.23	3.20
13	10.46	8.83	7.40	6.60	5.96	4.83	3.71
14	11.47	9.72	8.20	7.35	6.66	5.44	4.23
15	12.48	10.63	9.00	8.10	7.37	6.07	4.78
16	13.50	11.54	9.82	8.87	8.09	6.72	5.33
17	14.52	12.46	10.65	9.65	8.83	7.37	5.91
18	15.54	13.38	11.49	10.43	9.57	8.04	6.49
19	16.57	14.31	12.33	11.23	10.33	8.72	7.09
20	17.61	15.24	13.18	12.03	11.09	9.41	7.70
21	18.65	16.18	14.03	12.83	11.85	10.10	8.31
22	19.69	17.13	14.89	13.65	12.63	10.81	8.94
23	20.73	18.07	15.76	14.47	13.41	11.52	9.58
24	21.78	19.03	16.63	15.29	14.20	12.24	10.22
25	22.83	19.98	17.50	16.12	14.99	12.96	10.88
26	23.88	20.94	18.38	16.95	15.79	13.70	11.53
27	24.93	21.90	19.26	17.79	16.59	14.43	12.20
28	25.99	22.86	20.15	18.64	17.40	15.18	12.88
29	27.05	23.83	21.03	19.48	18.21	15.93	13.56
30	28.11	24.80	21.93	20.33	19.03	16.68	14.24
31	29.17	25.77	22.82	21.19	19.85	17.44	14.93
32	30.23	26.74	23.72	22.04	20.67	18.20	15.63
33	31.30	27.72	24.62	22.90	21.50	18.97	16.33
34	32.36	28.69	25.52	23.77	22.33	19.74	17.04
35	33.43	29.67	26.43	24.63	23.16	20.51	17.75
36	34.50	30.65	27.34	25.50	24.00	21.29	18.46
37	35.57	31.63	28.25	26.37	24.84	22.07	19.18
38	36.64	32.62	29.16	27.25	25.68	22.86	19.91
39	37.71	33.60	30.08	28.12	26.53	23.65	20.63

continued overleaf

Table 10.4 (*continued*)

N	Probability of blocking a connection						
	0.1	0.05	0.02	0.01	0.005	0.001	0.0001
	Offered traffic in Erlangs:						
40	38.78	34.59	30.99	29.00	27.38	24.44	21.37
41	39.86	35.58	31.91	29.88	28.23	25.23	22.10
42	40.93	36.57	32.83	30.77	29.08	26.03	22.84
43	42.01	37.56	33.75	31.65	29.93	26.83	23.58
44	43.08	38.55	34.68	32.54	30.79	27.64	24.33
45	44.16	39.55	35.60	33.43	31.65	28.44	25.08
46	45.24	40.54	36.53	34.32	32.51	29.25	25.83
47	46.32	41.54	37.46	35.21	33.38	30.06	26.58
48	47.40	42.53	38.39	36.10	34.24	30.87	27.34
49	48.48	43.53	39.32	37.00	35.11	31.69	28.10
50	49.56	44.53	40.25	37.90	35.98	32.51	28.86
55	54.9	49.5	44.9	42.4	40.3	36.6	32.7
60	60.4	54.5	49.6	46.9	44.7	40.7	36.6
65	65.8	59.6	54.3	51.5	49.1	44.9	40.5
70	71.2	64.6	59.1	56.1	53.6	49.2	44.5
75	76.7	69.7	63.9	60.7	58.1	53.5	48.6
80	82.2	74.8	68.6	65.3	62.6	57.8	52.6
85	87.6	79.9	73.4	70.0	67.2	62.1	56.7
90	93.1	85.0	78.3	74.6	71.7	66.4	60.9
95	98.6	90.1	83.1	79.3	76.3	70.8	65.0
100	104.1	95.2	87.9	84.0	80.9	75.2	69.2
105	109.5	100.3	92.8	88.7	85.5	79.6	73.4
110	115.0	105.4	97.6	93.4	90.1	84.0	77.6
115	120.5	110.6	102.5	98.2	94.7	88.5	81.9
120	126.0	115.7	107.4	102.9	99.3	92.9	86.2
125	131.5	120.9	112.3	107.7	104.0	97.4	90.4
130	137.0	126.0	117.1	112.4	108.6	101.9	94.7
135	142.5	131.2	122.0	117.2	113.3	106.4	99.0
140	148.1	136.3	126.9	122.0	118.0	110.9	103.4
145	153.6	141.5	131.8	126.7	122.7	115.4	107.7
150	159.1	146.7	136.8	131.5	127.3	119.9	112.1
155	164.6	151.8	141.7	136.3	132.0	124.4	116.4
160	170.1	157.0	146.6	141.1	136.7	129.0	120.8
165	175.6	162.2	151.5	145.9	141.5	133.5	125.2
170	181.1	167.3	156.4	150.7	146.2	138.1	129.6
175	186.7	172.5	161.4	155.5	150.9	142.6	134.0
180	192.2	177.7	166.3	160.4	155.6	147.2	138.4
185	197.7	182.9	171.3	165.2	160.4	151.8	142.8
190	203.2	188.1	176.2	170.0	165.1	156.4	147.2
195	208.7	193.3	181.2	174.9	169.8	161.0	151.7
200	214.0	198.5	186.1	179.7	174.6	165.6	156.1

This is three orders of magnitude better than for the maximum number of connections.

As an alternative to using Figure 10.10, a traffic table based on Erlang's lost call formula is provided in Table 10.4.

So, we have seen that, for both CBR and VBR traffic, when the connection blocking probability requirements are taken into account, the actual cell loss probability can be rather lower than that for the maximum allowed number of connections.

11 Priority Control

the customer comes first

11.1 PRIORITIES

ATM networks can feature two forms of priority mechanism: space and time. Both forms relate to how an ATM buffer operates, and these are illustrated in Figure 11.1. Space priority addresses whether or not a cell is admitted into the finite waiting area of the buffer. Time priority deals with the order in which cells leave the waiting area and enter the server for onward transmission. Thus the main focus for the space priority mechanism is to distinguish different levels of cell loss performance, whereas for time priority the focus is on the delay performance. For both forms of priority, the waiting area can be organised in different ways, depending on the specific priority algorithm being implemented.

The ATM standards explicitly support space priority, by the provision of a cell loss priority bit in the ATM cell header. High priority is indicated by the cell loss priority bit having a value of 0; low priority with a value of 1. Different levels of time priority, however, are not explicitly supported in the standards. One way they can be organised is by assigning different levels of time priority to particular VPI/VCI values or ranges of values.

11.2 SPACE PRIORITY AND THE CELL LOSS PRIORITY BIT

An ATM terminal distinguishes the level of space priority for the traffic flows it is generating by setting the value of the cell loss priority bit.

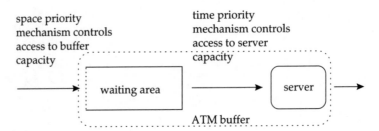

space priority
mechanism controls
access to buffer
capacity

time priority
mechanism controls
access to server
capacity

waiting area   server

ATM buffer

Figure 11.1
Space and time priority mechanisms

the buffer is full with a mix of high
and low priority cells and another
high priority cell arrives

H 6 → H 5 L H 4 H 3 H 2 L H 1   server

ATM buffer

the last low priority cell is "pushed
out" of the buffer, providing room
for the arriving high priority cell

H 6 H 5 H 4 H 3 H 2 L H 1   server

ATM buffer

Figure 11.2
Space priority: the push-out scheme

Within the network, if buffer overflow occurs, the network elements may selectively discard cells of the lower priority flow in order to maintain the performance objectives required of both the high and low priority traffic. For example, a terminal producing compressed video can use high priority for the important synchronisation information. This then avoids the need to operate the network elements, through which the video connection is routed, at extremely low levels of cell loss probability, for all the cells in the connection. The priority mechanism is able to achieve a very low loss probability, just for those cells that require it, and this leads to a significant improvement in the traffic load that can be admitted to the network.

Two selective cell discarding schemes have been proposed and studied for ATM buffers: the push-out scheme; and partial buffer sharing. The push-out scheme is illustrated in Figure 11.2; an arriving cell of high

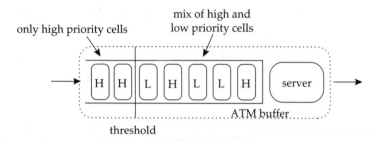

Figure 11.3
Space priority: partial buffer sharing

priority which finds the buffer full *replaces* a low priority cell within the buffer. If the buffer contains only high priority cells, then the arriving cell is discarded. A low priority cell arriving to find a full buffer is always discarded. The partial buffer sharing scheme (see Figure 11.3), reserves a part of the buffer for high priority cells only. If the queue is below a threshold size, then both low and high priority cells are accepted onto the queue. Above the threshold only high priority cells are accepted.

The push-out scheme achieves only slightly better performance than partial buffer sharing. But the buffer management and implementation are rather more complex for the push-out mechanism because, when a high priority cell arrives to a full buffer, a low priority cell in the buffer must be found and discarded. Thus the partial buffer sharing scheme achieves the best compromise between performance and complexity. Let's look at how partial buffer sharing can be analysed, so we can quantify the improvements in admissible load that are possible with space priorities.

11.3 PARTIAL BUFFER SHARING

An analysis of the partial buffer sharing scheme is possible for the sort of queueing system in Chapter 5: a synchronised server, a finite buffer, and Poisson input (a synchronised $M/D/1/X$ queue). Here, we will use the line crossing form of analysis (see Chapter 7) as this allows a relatively simple approach.

In Chapter 5, the input traffic is a batch arrival process, where the size of a batch can vary from cell slot to cell slot, described by a probability distribution for the number of cells in the batch. This allows the queue to be analysed for arbitrary distributions, and in Chapter 5 results are shown for Poisson and binomial distributions.

For the analysis of an ATM buffer with partial buffer sharing, we restrict the input to be a Poisson distributed batch, comprising two streams of traffic: one for each level of space priority. We define the probability that there are k arrivals in one slot as

$$a(k) = \frac{a^k}{k!}e^{-a}$$

where the mean arrival rate (in cells per cell slot) is given by parameter a. This mean arrival rate is the sum of mean arrival rates, a_h and a_l, for the high and low priority streams respectively:

$$a = a_h + a_l$$

and so we can define the probability that there are k high priority arrivals in one slot as

$$a_h(k) = \frac{a_h^k}{k!}e^{-a_h}$$

and the probability that there are k low priority arrivals in one slot as

$$a_l(k) = \frac{a_l^k}{k!}e^{-a_l}$$

The probability of the queueing system being in state k is defined as

$s(k) = \Pr\{$there are k cells, of either priority, in the system at the end of a slot$\}$

The maximum number of cells in the system, i.e. the waiting area and the server, is X, and the maximum number of low priority cells, i.e. the threshold level, is M, where $M < X$. Below the threshold level, cells of either priority are admitted into the buffer.

Equating the probabilities of crossing the line between states 0 and 1 gives

$$s(1)a(0) = s(0)(1 - a(0))$$

where the left hand side gives the probability of crossing down (one cell in the queue, which is served, and no arrivals), and the right hand side gives the probability of crossing up (no cells in the queue, and one or more cells arrive). Remember that any arrivals during the current time slot cannot be served during this slot. Rearranging the equation gives

$$s(1) = \frac{s(0)(1 - a(0))}{a(0)}$$

In general, equating the probabilities of crossing the line between states $k - 1$ and k, for $k < M$, gives

$$s(k)a(0) = s(0)A(k) + \sum_{i=1}^{k-1} s(i)A(k - i + 1)$$

where $A(k)$ is the probability that at least k cells arrive during the time slot, and is expressed simply as the probability that fewer than k cells do not arrive.

$$A(k) = 1 - \sum_{j=0}^{k-1} a(j)$$

$A_h(k)$ is the probability that at least k high priority cells arrive during a time slot, and is defined in a similar manner in terms of $a_h(j)$; this is used later on in the analysis.

So, in general for $k < M$, we have

$$s(k) = \frac{s(0)A(k) + \sum_{i=1}^{k-1} s(i)A(k - i + 1)}{a(0)}$$

Continuing the analysis for state probabilities $s(k)$ at or above $k = M$ is not so straightforward, because the order in which the cells arrive in the buffer is important if the system is changing from a state below the threshold to a state above the threshold.

Consider the case in which a buffer, with a threshold $M = 10$ cells and system capacity $X = 20$ cells, has eight cells in the system at the end of a time slot. During the next time slot, four low priority cells and two high priority cells arrive, and one cell is served. If the low priority cells arrive first, then two low priority cells are admitted, taking the system up to the threshold, the other two low priority cells are discarded, and the two high priority cells are admitted, taking the system size to 12. Then the cell in the server completes service and the system size reduces to 11, which is the system state at the end of this time slot. If the high priority cells arrive first, then these take the system up to the threshold size of 10, and so all four low priority cells are discarded. At the end of the slot the system size is then nine (the cell in the server completes service).

To analyse how the system changes from one state to another we need to know the number of cells that are *admitted* onto the buffer (at a later stage we will be interested in the number of cells that are *not* admitted, in order to calculate the loss from the system). So, let's say that $m + n$ cells are admitted out of a total of i cells that arrive during one cell slot. Of those admitted, the first m are of either high or low priority and take the system from its current state up to the threshold level, and then the other n are of high priority. Thus $i - (m + n)$ low priority cells are lost. We use the following expression for the probability that these $m + n$ cells are admitted:

$$a'(m, n) = \sum_{i=m+n}^{\infty} \left[a(i) \frac{(i - m)!}{n!(i - m - n)!} \left(\frac{a_h}{a} \right)^n \left(\frac{a_l}{a} \right)^{i-m-n} \right]$$

The binomial part of the expression determines the probability that, of the $i - m$ cells to arrive when the queue is at or above the threshold, n are high priority cells. Here, the probability that a cell is of high priority is expressed as the proportion of the mean arrival rate that is of high priority. Note that, although this expression is an infinite summation, it converges rapidly and so needs only a few terms to obtain a value for $a'(m, n)$.

With the line crossing analysis, we need to express the probability that m cells of either priority arrive, and then at least n or more high priority cells arrive, denoted $A'(m, n)$. This can be expressed as

$$A'(m, n) = \sum_{j=n}^{\infty} a'(m, j)$$

Another way of expressing this is by working out the probability that fewer than $m + n$ cells are admitted. This happens in two different ways: either the total number of cells arriving during a slot is not enough, or there are enough cells, but the order in which they arrive is such that there are not enough high priority cells above the threshold.

$$A'(m, n) = 1 - \sum_{i=0}^{m+n-1} a(i)$$

$$- \sum_{i=0}^{\infty} \left[a(m + n + i) \sum_{j=0}^{n-1} \left\{ \frac{(n + i)!}{j!(n + i - j)!} \left(\frac{a_h}{a} \right)^j \left(\frac{a_l}{a} \right)^{n+i-j} \right\} \right]$$

We can now analyse the system at or above the threshold. Equating probabilities of crossing the line between M and $M - 1$ gives

$$s(M) a_h(0) = s(0) A(M) + \sum_{i=1}^{M-1} s(i) A'(M - i, 1)$$

The left hand side is the probability of crossing down; to stay at the threshold level, or to move above it, at least one high priority cell is needed, so the state reduces by one only if there are no high priority arrivals. The right hand side is the probability of crossing up from below the threshold. The first term is for crossing up from the state when there is nothing in the system; this requires M, or more, cells of either priority. The second term is for all the non-zero states, i, below the threshold; in these cases there is always a cell in the server which leaves the system after any arrivals have been admitted to the queue. Thus at least one high priority arrival is required after there have been sufficient arrivals $(M - i)$ of either priority to fill the queue up to the threshold.

For $k > M$, we have

$$s(k)a_h(0) = s(0)A'(M, k - M) + \sum_{i=1}^{M-1}\{s(i)A'(M - i, k - M + 1)\}$$
$$+ \sum_{i=M}^{k-1}\{s(i)A_h(k - i + 1)\}$$

This differs from the situation for $k = M$ in two respects: firstly, the crossing up from state 0 requires M cells of either priority and a further $k - M$ of high priority; and secondly, it is now possible to cross the line from a state at or above the threshold — this can only be achieved with high priority arrivals.

At the buffer limit, $k = X$, we have only one way of reaching this state: from state 0, with M cells of either priority followed by at least $X - M$ cells of high priority. If there is at least one cell in the queue at the start of the slot, and enough arrivals fill the queue, then at the end of the slot, the cell in the server will complete service and take the queue state from X down to $X - 1$. Thus for $k = X$ we have

$$s(X)a_h(0) = s(0)A'(M, X - M)$$

Now, as in Chapter 5, we have no value for $s(0)$, so we cannot evaluate $s(k)$ for $k > 0$. Therefore we define a new variable, $u(k)$, as

$$u(k) = \frac{s(k)}{s(0)}$$

so

$$u(0) = 1$$

Then

$$u(1) = \frac{(1 - a(0))}{a(0)}$$

For $1 < k < M$

$$u(k) = \frac{A(k) + \sum\limits_{i=1}^{k-1} u(i)A(k - i + 1)}{a(0)}$$

At the threshold

$$u(M) = \frac{A(M) + \sum\limits_{i=1}^{M-1} u(i)A'(M - i, 1)}{a_h(0)}$$

For $M < k < X - 1$

$$u(k) = \frac{A'(M, k - M) + \sum\limits_{i=1}^{M-1} \{u(i)A'(M - i, k - M + 1)\} + \sum\limits_{i=M}^{k-1} \{u(i)A_h(k - i + 1)\}}{a_h(0)}$$

At the system capacity

$$u(X) = \frac{A'(M, X - M)}{a_h(0)}$$

All the values of $u(k), 0 \leqslant k \leqslant X$, can be evaluated. Then, as in Chapter 5, we can calculate the probability that the system is empty:

$$s(0) = \frac{1}{\sum\limits_{i=0}^{X} u(i)}$$

and from that, find the rest of the state probability distribution:

$$s(k) = s(0)u(k)$$

Before we go on to calculate the cell loss probability for the high and low priority cell streams, let's first show an example state probability distribution for an ATM buffer implementing the partial buffer sharing scheme. Figure 11.4 shows the state probabilities when the buffer capacity is 20 cells, and the threshold level is 15 cells, for three different loads: (i) the low priority load, a_l, is 0.7 and the high priority load, a_h, is 0.175 of the cell slot rate; (ii) $a_l = 0.6$ and $a_h = 0.15$; and (iii) $a_l = 0.5$ and $a_h = 0.125$.

The graph shows a clear distinction between the gradients of the state probability distribution below and above the threshold level. Below the

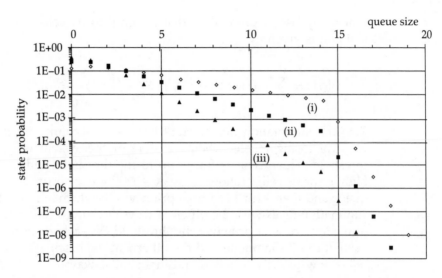

Figure 11.4
State probability distribution for ATM buffer with partial buffer sharing (i) $a_l = 0.7$, $a_h = 0.175$, (ii) $a_l = 0.6$, $a_h = 0.15$, (iii) $a_l = 0.5$, $a_h = 0.125$

threshold, the queue behaves like an ordinary $M/D/1$ with a gradient corresponding to the combined high and low priority load. Above the threshold, only the high priority cell stream has any effect, and so the gradient is much steeper because the load on this part of the queue is much less.

In Chapter 5, the loss probability was found by comparing the offered and the carried traffic at the cell level. But now we have two different priority streams, and the partial buffer sharing analysis only gives the combined carried traffic. The *overall* cell loss probability can be found using

$$\text{CLP} = \frac{a_l + a_h - (1 - s(0))}{a_l + a_h}$$

But the main objective of having a space priority scheme is to provide different levels of cell loss. How can we calculate this cell loss probability for each priority stream? It has to be done by considering the probability of losing a group of low or high priority cells during a cell slot, and then taking the weighted mean over all the possible group sizes. The high priority cell loss probability is given by

$$\text{CLP}_h = \frac{\sum_j j l_h(j)}{a_h}$$

where $l_h(j)$ is the probability that j high priority cells are lost in a cell slot and is given by

$$l_h(j) = \sum_{i=0}^{M-1} s(i)a'(M-i, X-M+j) + \sum_{i=M}^{X} s(i)a_h(X-i+j)$$

The first summation on the right hand side accounts for the different ways of losing j cells when the state of the system is less than the threshold. This involves filling up to the threshold with either low or high priority cells, followed by $X - M$ high priority cells to fill the queue and then a further j high priority cells which are lost. The second summation deals with the different ways of losing j cells when the state of the system is at or above the threshold; $X - i$ high priority cells are needed to fill the queue and the other j in the batch are lost.

The low priority loss is found in a similar way:

$$CLP_l = \frac{\sum_j jl_l(j)}{a_l}$$

where $l_l(j)$ is the probability that j low priority cells are lost in a cell slot and is given by

$$l_l(j) = \sum_{i=0}^{M-1} \left[s(i) \sum_{r=M-i+j}^{\infty} a(r) \frac{(r-(M-i))!}{(r-(M-i)-j)!j!} \left(\frac{a_h}{a}\right)^{r-(M-i)-j} \left(\frac{a_l}{a}\right)^j \right]$$

$$+ \sum_{i=M}^{X} s(i)a_l(j)$$

The first term on the right hand side accounts for the different ways of losing j cells when the state of the system is less than the threshold. This involves filling up to the threshold with either $M - i$ cells of either low or high priority, followed by any number of high priority cells along with j low priority cells (which are lost). The second summation deals with the different ways of losing j cells when the state of the system is above the threshold. This is simply the probability of j low priority cells arriving in a time slot, for each of the states at or above the threshold.

Increasing the admissible load

Let's now demonstrate the effect of introducing a partial buffer sharing mechanism to an ATM buffer. Suppose we have a buffer of size $X = 20$, and the most stringent cell loss probability requirement for traffic through the buffer is 10^{-10}. From Table 8.1 we find that the maximum admissible load is 0.521. Now the traffic mix is such that there is a high priority load of 0.125 which requires the CLP of 10^{-10}; the rest of the traffic can tolerate a CLP of 10^{-3}, a margin of seven orders of magnitude. Without a space priority mechanism, a maximum load of $0.521 - 0.125 = 0.396$ of this other traffic can be admitted. However, the partial buffer sharing analysis shows that, with a threshold of $M = 15$, the low priority load can be increased to 0.7 to give a cell loss probability of 1.16×10^{-3}, and the high priority load of 0.125 has a cell loss probability of 9.36×10^{-11}. The total admissible load has increased by just over 30% of the cell slot rate, from 0.521 to 0.825, representing a 75% increase in the low priority traffic.

If the threshold is set to $M = 18$, the low priority load can only be increased to 0.475 giving a cell loss probability of 5.6×10^{-8}, and the high priority load of 0.125 has a cell loss probability of 8.8×10^{-11}. But even this is an extra 8% of the cell slot rate, representing an increase in 20% for the low priority traffic, for a cell loss margin of between two and three orders of magnitude. Thus a substantial increase in load is possible, particularly if the difference in cell loss probability requirement is large.

Dimensioning buffers for partial buffer sharing

Figures 11.5 and 11.6 show interesting results from the partial buffer sharing analysis. In both cases, the high priority load is fixed at 0.125, and the space above the threshold is held constant at five cells. In Figure 11.5, the low priority load is varied from 0.4 up to 0.8, and the cell loss probability results are plotted for the high and low priority traffic against the combined load. This is done for three different buffer capacities. The results show that the margin in the cell loss probabilities is almost constant, at seven orders of magnitude. Figure 11.6 shows the same margin in the cell loss probabilities for a total load of 0.925 ($a_h = 0.125$, $a_l = 0.8$) as the buffer capacity is varied from 10 cells up to 50 cells.

The difference in high and low priority cell loss is almost invariant to the buffer capacity and the total load, provided that the space above the threshold, and the high priority load, are kept constant. Table 11.1 shows how the margin varies with the space above the threshold, and the high priority load (note that margins greater than 11 orders of magnitude are not included — these are unlikely to be required in practice). The values are also plotted in Figure 11.7.

With this information, buffers can be dimensioned using the following procedure:

1. Set the threshold by using Table 8.1 based on the $M/D/1/X$ analysis (without priorities) for the combined load and the combined cell

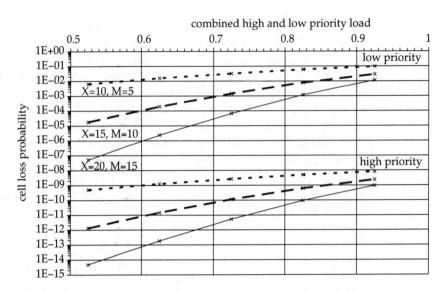

Figure 11.5
Low and high priority cell loss against load, for $X - M = 5$ and $a_h = 0.125$

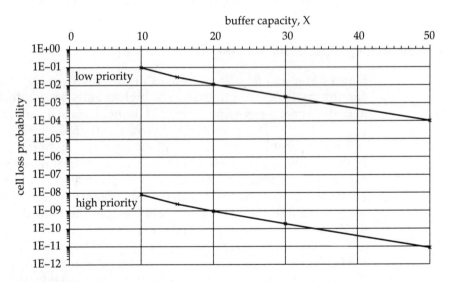

Figure 11.6
Low and high priority cell loss against buffer capacity, for $a = 0.925$ and $X - M = 5$

loss probability requirement. The latter is found using the following relationship (which is based on equating the average number of cells lost per cell slot):

$$CLP = \frac{a_l \, CLP_l + a_h \, CLP_h}{a}$$

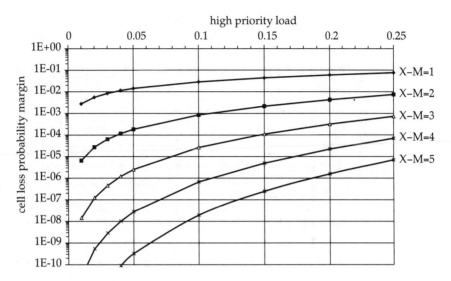

Figure 11.7
Cell loss probability margin against high priority load for different values of
$X - M$

Table 11.1
Cell loss probability margin between low and high priority traffic

$X - M$	High priority traffic load (as a fraction of the cell slot rate)								
	0.01	0.02	0.03	0.04	0.05	0.1	0.15	0.2	0.25
1	2.7E-03	5.6E-03	8.4E-03	1.1E-02	1.4E-02	2.8E-02	4.4E-02	5.9E-02	7.6E-02
2	6.5E-06	2.7E-05	6.3E-05	1.2E-04	1.8E-04	8.4E-04	2.2E-03	4.3E-03	7.5E-03
3	1.4E-08	1.2E-07	4.5E-07	1.2E-06	2.5E-06	2.6E-05	1.1E-04	3.2E-04	7.4E-04
4	3.0E-11	5.4E-10	2.9E-09	1.0E-08	2.8E-08	6.7E-07	4.9E-06	2.2E-05	7.0E-05
5	—	—	1.8E-11	9.0E-11	3.3E-10	1.9E-08	2.5E-07	1.6E-06	7.0E-06

2. Add buffer space above the threshold determined by the high
   priority load and the additional cell loss probability margin, from
   Table 11.1.

Let's take an example. We have a requirement for a buffer to carry a
total load of 0.7, with low priority CLP of 10^{-6} and high priority CLP of
10^{-10}. The high priority load is 0.15. Thus the overall CLP is given by

$$CLP = \frac{0.55 \times 10^{-6} + 0.15 \times 10^{-10}}{0.7} = 7.86 \times 10^{-7}$$

From Table 8.1 we find that the threshold is between 20 and 25 cells, but
closer to 20; we will use $M = 21$. Table 11.1 gives an additional buffer
space of three cells for a margin of 10^{-4} and high priority load of 0.15.
Thus the total buffer capacity is 24. If we put these values of $X = 24$

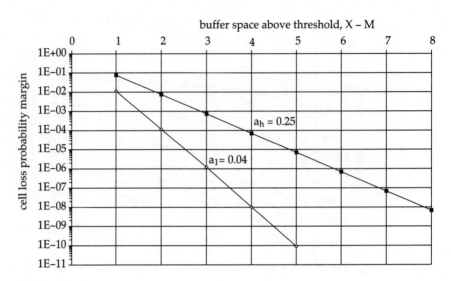

Figure 11.8
Cell loss probability margin against buffer space reserved for high priority traffic, X − M

and $M = 21$, $a_l = 0.55$ and $a_h = 0.15$ back into the analysis, the results are $CLP_l = 5.5 \times 10^{-7}$ and $CLP_h = 6.3 \times 10^{-11}$. For a buffer size of 23, a threshold of 20, and the same load, the results are $CLP_l = 1.1 \times 10^{-6}$ and $CLP_h = 1.2 \times 10^{-10}$.

Two of the values for high priority load in Table 11.1 are of particular interest in the development of a useful dimensioning rule; these values are 0.04 and 0.25. In Figure 11.8, the CLP margin is plotted against the buffer space above the threshold (this is shown as a continuous line to illustrate the log-lin relationship — the buffer space of course varies in integer values). At the 25% load, each cell space reserved for high priority traffic is worth one order of magnitude on the CLP margin. At the 4% load, it is two orders of magnitude. We can express this as

$$CLP_{margin} = 10^{-(X-M)}$$

for a high priority load of 25% of the cell slot rate, and

$$CLP_{margin} = 10^{-2(X-M)}$$

for a high priority load of 4% of the cell slot rate.

11.4   TIME PRIORITY IN ATM

In order to demonstrate the operation of time priorities, let's define two traffic classes, of high and low time priority. In a practical system, there

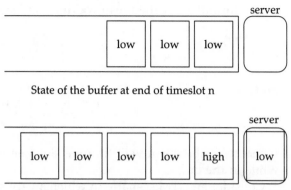

State of the buffer at end of timeslot n

State of the buffer at end of timeslot n+1 after 3 cells
have arrived — one of high priority and two of low priority

Figure 11.9
Time priorities in ATM

may be rather more levels, according to the perceived traffic requirements. The ATM buffer in Figure 11.9 operates in such a way that any
high priority cells are always served before any low priority. Thus a high
priority cell arriving at a buffer with only low priority cells currently
in the queue will go straight to the head of the queue. Note that at the
beginning of time slot $n + 1$ the low priority cell currently at the head
of the queue goes into service. It is only during time slot $n + 1$ that the
high priority cell arrives and is then placed at the head of the queue.
The same principle can be applied with many levels of priority. Note
that any cell arriving to find the buffer full is lost, regardless of the level
of time priority.

The effect of time priorities is to decrease the delay for the higher
priority traffic at the expense of increasing the delays for the lower
priority traffic. As far as ATM is concerned, this means that real time
connections (e.g. voice and interactive video) can be speeded on their
way at the expense of delaying the cells of connections which do not
have real time constraints, e.g. data.

To analyse the delay performance for a system with two levels of
time priority, we will assume an $M/D/1$ system, with infinite buffer
length. Although time priorities do affect the cell loss performance, we
will concentrate on those analytical results that apply to *delay*.

Mean value analysis

We define the mean arrival rate in cells per slot as a_i for cells of priority
i. High priority is indicated by $i = 1$ and low priority by $i = 2$. Note
that the following analysis can be extended to many levels if required.

The formulas for the mean waiting time are:

$$w_1 = \frac{a_1 + a_2}{2(1 - a_1)}$$

and

$$w_2 = \frac{w_1 a_1 + [(a_1 + a_2)/2]}{1 - a_1 - a_2}$$

where w_i is the mean wait (in time slots) endured by cells of priority i while in the buffer.

Consider an ATM scenario in which a very small proportion of traffic, say about 1%, is given high time priority. Figure 11.10 shows the effect on the mean waiting times. Granting a time priority to a small proportion of traffic has very little effect on the mean wait for the lower priority traffic, which is indistinguishable from the mean wait when there are no priorities. We can also see from the results that the waiting time for the high priority cells is greatly improved.

Figure 11.11 shows what happens if the proportion of high priority traffic is significantly increased, to 50% of the combined high and low priority load. Even in this situation, mean waiting times for the low priority cells are not severely affected, and waiting times for the priority traffic have still been noticeably improved. Figure 11.12 illustrates the case when most of the traffic is high priority and only 1% is of low priority. Here, there is little difference between the no priority case and

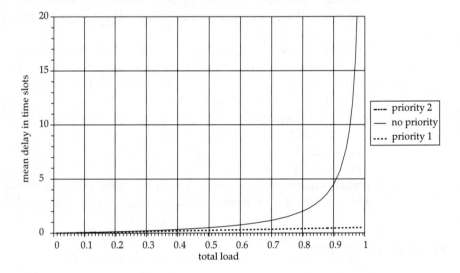

Figure 11.10
Mean waiting time for high and low time priority traffic, where the proportion of high priority traffic is 1% of the total load

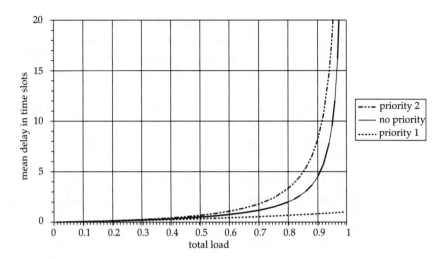

Figure 11.11
Mean waiting time for high and low time priority traffic, where the proportion of high priority traffic is 50% of the total load

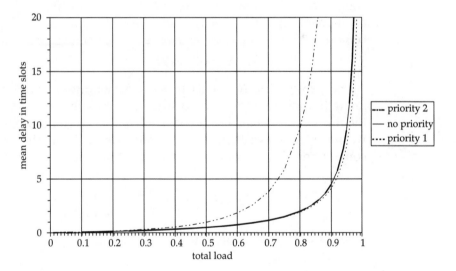

Figure 11.12
Mean waiting time for high and low time priority traffic, where the proportion of high priority traffic is 99% of the total load

the results for the high priority traffic, but the very small amount of low priority traffic has significantly worse waiting times.

The results so far are for the *mean* waiting time. Let's now consider the effect of time priorities on the *distribution* of the waiting time. To find the waiting time probabilities for cells in an ATM buffer where different levels of time priority are present requires the use of convolution (as indeed did finding waiting times in a non-priority buffer — see Chapter 5). A cell, say **C**, arriving in timeslot i will wait behind a number of cells, and this number has four components:

1. The total number of cells of equal or higher priority that are present in the buffer at the end of timeslot $i - 1$
2. The number of cells of the *same priority* that are ahead of **C** in the batch in which **C** arrives
3. All the cells of higher priority than **C** that arrive in timeslot i
4. Higher priority cells that arrive subsequently, but before **C** enters service.

Again, if we focus on just two levels of priority, we can find the probability that a cell of low priority (priority 2) has to wait k time slots before it can enter service, by finding expressions for the four individual components. Let us define:

component   1 — the unfinished work — as $u(k)$
component   2 — the "batch wait" — as $b(k)$
component   3 — the wait caused by priority 1 arrivals in time slot
            i — as $a_1(k)$

Then, excluding the effect of subsequent high priority arrivals, we know that our waiting time distribution must be (in part) the sum of the three components listed above. Note that to sum random variables, we must convolve their distributions. We will call the result of this convolution the "virtual waiting time distribution", $v(k)$, given by:

$$v(\cdot) = u(\cdot) * b(\cdot) * a_1(\cdot)$$

where $*$ denotes convolution. We can rewrite this as:

$$v(k) = \sum_{i=0}^{k} \left[u(k-i) \sum_{j=0}^{i} b(j)a_1(i-j) \right]$$

But where do the three distributions, $u(k)$, $b(k)$ and $a_1(k)$ come from? As we are assuming Poisson arrivals for both priorities, $a_1(k)$ is simply:

$$a_1(k) = \frac{a_1^k}{k!} e^{-a_1}$$

and for the low priority cells we will have:

$$a_2(k) = \frac{a_2^k}{k!}e^{-a_2}$$

where

    a_1 is the arrival rate (in cells per time slot) of high priority cells
    a_2 is the arrival rate (in cells per time slot) of low priority cells

The unfinished work, $u(k)$, is actually found from the state probabilities, denoted $s(k)$, the formula for which was given in Chapter 5:

$$u(0) = s(0) + s(1)$$

$$u(k) = s(k+1) \qquad \text{for } k > 0$$

What about the wait caused by other cells of low priority arriving in the same batch, but in front of C? Well there is a simple approach here too:

$$b(k) = \Pr\{\text{C is } (k+1)^{\text{th}} \text{ in the batch}\}$$

$$= \frac{\text{E [number of cells that are } (k+1)^{\text{th}} \text{ in their batch]}}{\text{E [number of cells arriving per slot]}}$$

$$= \frac{1 - \sum\limits_{i=0}^{k} a_2(i)}{a_2}$$

So now all the parts are assembled, and we need only implement the convolution to find the virtual waiting time distribution. However, this still leaves us with the problem of accounting for subsequent high priority arrivals. In fact this is very easy to do using a formula developed (originally) for an entirely different purpose. The result is that:

$$w(0) = v(0)$$

$$w(k) = \frac{\sum\limits_{i=1}^{k} v(i)a_1(k-i,k)i}{k} \qquad \text{for } k > 0$$

where:

    $w(k) = \Pr\{\text{a priority 2 cell must wait } k \text{ time slots before it enters service}\}$

$$a_1(k,x) = \frac{(xa_1)^k}{k!}e^{-xa_1}$$

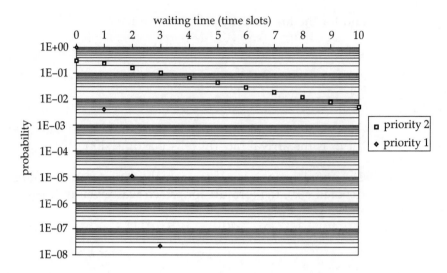

Figure 11.13
Waiting time distribution for high and low time priority traffic, where the proportion of high priority traffic is 1% of a total load of 0.8 cells per time slot

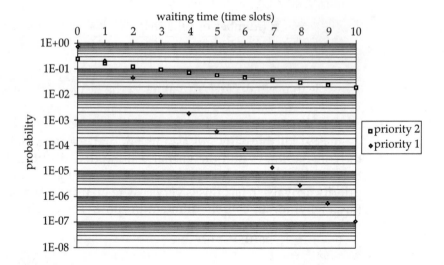

Figure 11.14
Waiting time distribution for high and low time priority traffic, where the proportion of high priority traffic is 50% of a total load of 0.8 cells per time slot

So $a_1(k, x)$ is simply the probability that k priority 1 cells arrive in x time slots.

Figure 11.13 and Figure 11.14 show the waiting time distributions for high and low priority cells when the combined load is 0.8 cells per time slot and the high priority proportion is 1% and 50% respectively. From

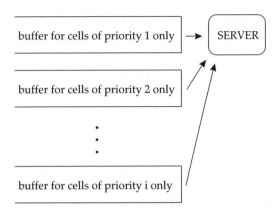

Figure 11.15
Practical arrangement of priority buffers at an output port

these results, it is clear that, even for a relatively large proportion of high priority traffic, the effect on the waiting time distribution for low priority traffic is small, but the benefits to the high priority traffic are significant.

Before we leave time priorities, it is worth noting that practical systems for implementing them would probably feature a buffer for each priority level, as shown in Figure 11.15, rather than one buffer for all priorities as in Figure 11.9. Although there is no explicit provision in the standards for distinguishing different levels of time priority, it is possible to use the VPI/VCI values in the header. On entry to a switch, the VPI/VCI values are used to determine the outgoing port required, so it is a relatively simple extension to use these values to choose one of a number of time priority buffers at that output port.

Using one buffer per priority level (Figure 11.15) would have little effect on the delays experienced by the cells but it would affect the CLP. This is because, for a given total capacity of X cells, the CLP is minimised if the total space is shared amongst the different priorities (as in Figure 11.9). However, this has to be balanced against considerations of extra complexity (and hence cost) inherent in a buffer sharing arrangement.

12 Fundamentals of ATM simulation

those vital statistics

12.1 DISCRETE TIME SIMULATION

This chapter is intended as an *introduction* to simulation and, in particular, its application to ATM. For anyone wanting a more comprehensive treatment of the subject of simulation in general, we refer to [3].

We will introduce the subject of ATM simulation by concentrating on a discrete version of the $M/D/1$ queue. There are two basic ways to simulate such a queue:

- discrete *time* advance
- discrete *event* advance

In the former, the simulator moves from time slot i to time slot $i+1$ regardless of whether the system state has changed, e.g. if the $M/D/1$ queue is empty at i it could still be empty at $i+1$ and the program will still only advance the clock to time $i+1$. In discrete event simulation, the simulator clock is advanced to the next time for which there is a change in the state of the simulation model, e.g. a cell arrival at the $M/D/1$ queue.

So we have a choice: discrete time advance or discrete event advance. The latter can run more quickly because it will cut out the slot to slot transitions when the queue is empty, but the former is easier to understand in the context of ATM because it is simpler to implement and it models the ATM buffer from the point of view of the server process, i.e.

the "conveyor belt" of cell slots (see Figure 1.4). We will concentrate on the discrete time advance mechanism in this introduction.

In the case of the synchronised $M/D/1$ queue the obvious events which the simulator can jump between are the end of time slot instants, and so the simulator needs to model the following algorithm:

$$K_i = \max(0, K_{i-1} + A_i - 1)$$

where

K_i = number of cells in modelled system at end of time slot i
A_i = number of cells arriving to the system during time slot i

This algorithm can be expressed as a simulation program in the following pseudocode:

```
BEGIN
    initialise variables
        i, A, K, arrival rate, time slot limit, histogram[]
    WHILE (i < time slot limit)
    generate new arrivals
        A := Poisson (arrival rate)
        K := K + A
    serve a waiting cell
        IF K > 0 THEN
            K := K − 1
        ELSE
            K := 0
    store results
        histogram [K] := histogram [K] + 1
    advance time to next time slot
        i := i + 1
    END WHILE
END
```

The main program loop implements the discrete time advance mechanism in the form of a loop counter, i. The beginning of the loop corresponds to the start of time slot i, and the first section "*generate new arrivals*" calls function "Poisson" which returns a random non-negative integer for the number of cell arrivals during this current time slot. As in Chapter 5, we model the queue with an arrivals first buffer management strategy, so the service instants occur at the end of the time slot after any arrivals. This is dealt with by the second section "*serve a waiting*

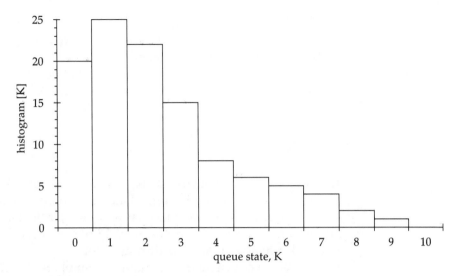

Figure 12.1
An example of a histogram of the queue state

cell" which decrements the queue state variable K, if it is greater than 0, i.e. if the queue is not empty. At this point, in *"store results"* we record the state of the queue in a histogram. This is simply a count of the number of times the queue is in state K, for each possible value of K, (see Figure 12.1) and can be converted to an estimate of the state probability distribution by dividing each value in the array "histogram[]" by the total number of time slots in the simulation run.

Generating random numbers

The function "Poisson" generates a random non-negative integer number of cell arrivals according to a Poisson distribution with a particular arrival rate. This is achieved in two parts: generate random numbers that are uniformly distributed over the range 0 to 1; convert these random numbers to be Poisson distributed. Let's assume that we have a function "generate random number" which implements the first part. The following pseudocode converts the random numbers from having a uniform distribution to having a Poisson distribution.

FUNCTION X = Poisson (arrival rate)
initialise variables
$\quad a := e^{-\text{arrivalrate}}$
$\quad b := 1$
$\quad j := -1$

REPEAT
    $j := j + 1$
    $U :=$ generate random number
    $b := bU$
UNTIL $(b < a)$
return result
    $X := j$
END FUNCTION

The REPEAT loop corresponds to the "generation" of cells, and the loop records the number of cells in the batch in variable j, returning the final total in variable X. Remember that with this particular simulation program we are not interested in the arrival time of each cell within the slot, but in the *number* of arrivals during a slot.

But how do we generate the random numbers themselves? A good random number generator (RNG) should produce a sequence of numbers which are uniformly distributed on the range [0, 1] and which do not exhibit any correlation between the generated numbers. It must be fast and avoid the need for much storage. An important property of the random number sequence is that it must be reproducible; this aids debugging, and can be used to increase the precision of the results.

A typical RNG is of the form:

$$U_i = (aU_{i-1} + c) \bmod (m)$$

where U_i is the ith random number generated, and m (the modulus), a (the multiplier), and c (the increment) are all non-negative integers, as is U_0, the initial value which is called the "seed". The values should satisfy $0 < m$, $a < m$, $c < m$ and $U_0 < m$. In practice m is chosen to be very large, say 10^9.

Obviously, once the RNG produces a value for U_i which it has produced before, the sequence of numbers being generated will repeat, and unwanted correlations will begin to appear in the simulator results. An important characteristic of a RNG is the length of the sequence before it repeats; this is called the period. The values of m and c are chosen, in part, to maximise this period. The Wichmann–Hill algorithm combines three of these basic generators to produce a random number generator which exhibits exceptional performance. The pseudocode for this algorithm is:

FUNCTION $U =$ generate random number
    $x := (171x) \bmod (30\,269)$
    $y := (172y) \bmod (30\,307)$

$z := (170z) \bmod (30\,323)$
$U := (x/30\,269) + (y/30\,307) + (z/30\,323)$
temp := trunc (U)
$U := U - \text{temp}$
END FUNCTION

The period is of particular relevance for ATM traffic studies, where rare events can occur with probabilities as low as 10^{-10} (e.g. lost cells). Once a RNG repeats its sequence, unwanted correlations will begin to appear in the results, depending on how the random number sequence has been applied. In our discrete time advance simulation, we are simulating time slot by time slot, where each time slot can have 0 or more cell arrivals. The RNG is called once per time slot, and then once for each cell arrival during the time slot. With the discrete event advance approach, a cell by cell simulator would call the RNG once per cell arrival to generate the inter-arrival time to the next cell.

The Wichmann–Hill algorithm has a period of about 7×10^{12}. Thus, so long as the number of cells and time slots does not exceed the period of 7×10^{12}, this RNG algorithm can be applied. The computing time required to simulate this number of cells is impractical anyway, so we can be confident that this RNG algorithm will not introduce correlation due to repetition of the random number sequence. Note that the period of the Wichmann–Hill algorithm is *significantly* better than many of the random number generators that are supplied in general purpose programming languages. So, check carefully before you use a built-in RNG.

Reaching steady state

When do we stop a simulation? This is not a trivial question, and if, for example, we want to find the cell loss probability in an $M/D/1/K$ model, then the probability we are seeking is actually a "steady state" probability: the long run proportion of cells lost during period T as $T \to \infty$. Since we cannot actually wait that long, we must have some prior idea about how long it takes for the simulator to reach a good approximation to steady state.

A simulation is said to be in steady state, not when the performance measurements become constant, but when the distribution of the measurements becomes (close to being) invariant with time. In particular, the simulation needs to be sufficiently long that the effect of the initial state of the system on the results is negligible. Let's take an example. Recall from Chapter 3 that we can use the probability that the queue size is greater than K, denoted $Q(K)$, as an estimate of the cell loss from a finite queue of size K. Suppose that the queue length is 2. We can calculate $Q(2)$ from the histogram data recorded in our simulation program thus:

$$Q(2) = \frac{\sum\limits_{K=3}^{\infty} \text{histogram } [K]}{i}$$

or, alternatively as

$$Q(2) = \frac{i - \sum\limits_{K=0}^{2} \text{histogram } [K]}{i}$$

If we start our $M/D/1$ simulator, and plot $Q(2)$ for it as this value evolves over time, we will see something like that shown in Figure 12.2.

Here, the simulator calculates a measurement result for $Q(2)$ every 1000 time slots; that is to say it provides an *estimate* of $Q(2)$ every 1000 slots. But from Figure 12.2 we can see that there are "transient" measurements, and that these strongly reflect the initial system state. It is possible to cut out these measurements in the calculation of steady state results, however it is not easy to identify when the transient phase is finished. We might consider the first 7000 slots as the transient period in our example.

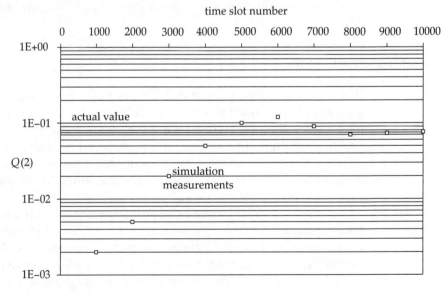

Figure 12.2
Evolution of Q(2) for the simulated M/D/1

Batch means and confidence intervals

The output from one run of a simulation is a sequence of measurements which depends on the particular sequence of random numbers used. In the example we have been considering, we store results at the end of each time slot, then, at intervals of 1000 time slots, we output a value for $Q(2)$. But we do not take the last value to be output as the final "result" of the simulation run. The *sequence* of measurements of $Q(2)$ needs to be evaluated statistically in order to provide reliable results for the steady state value of $Q(2)$.

Suppose that we take $j = 1$ to N measurements of $Q(2)$. Firstly, we can obtain an estimate of the mean value by calculating

$$\hat{Q}(2) = \frac{\sum\limits_{j=1}^{N} Q(2)_j}{N}$$

Then we need an estimate of how the measurements vary over the set. We can construct an estimate of the *confidence interval* for $Q(2)$ by calculating

$$\hat{Q}(2) + z_{\alpha/2} \frac{\sum\limits_{j=1}^{N} \left(Q(2)_j - \hat{Q}(2) \right)^2}{N(N-1)}$$

where $z_{\alpha/2}$ is obtained from standard normal tables and $1 - \alpha$ is the degree of confidence.

A confidence interval quantifies the confidence that can be ascribed to the results from a simulation experiment, in a statistical sense. For example, a 90% confidence interval (i.e. $\alpha = 0.1$) means that for 90% of the simulation runs for which an interval is calculated, the actual value for the measure of interest falls within the calculated interval (see Figure 12.3). On the other 10% of occasions, the actual value falls outside the calculated interval. The actual percentage of times that a confidence interval does span the correct value is called the coverage.

There are a number of different methods for organising simulation experiments so that confidence intervals can be calculated from the measurements. The method of independent replications uses N estimates obtained from N independent simulation runs. In the method of batch means, one single run is divided into N batches (each batch of a certain fixed number, L, of observations) from which N estimates are calculated. The value of L is crucial, because it determines the correlation between batches: considering our $M/D/1$ example again, if L is too small then the system state at the end of N_j will be heavily influenced

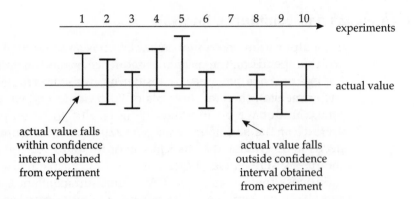

Figure 12.3
Confidence intervals and coverage

by (correlated with) the system state at the end of N_{j-1}. The regenerative method also uses a single run, but depends on the definition of a regenerative state — a state after which the process repeats probabilistically. Determining an appropriate regenerative state can be difficult, and it can be time consuming to obtain a sufficient number of points at which the simulation passes through such states, in order to calculate valid confidence intervals.

The main advantage of methods involving just a single run is that only one transient phase needs to be discarded. Determining the best length for the simulation run(s) is a problem for all three methods. This is because, if the runs are too short, they can produce confidence intervals with actual coverage considerably lower than desired. However, this has to be balanced against the need to limit the sample size to minimise the time (and hence, cost) of the simulation; so the emphasis is on finding a sufficient sample size. In addressing this problem, an alternative to the arbitrary fixed sample size approach is to increase the sample size sequentially until an acceptable confidence interval can be constructed.

Validation

Any simulation model will need to be checked to ensure that it works. This can be a problem: a very general program that is capable of analysing a large number of scenarios will be impossible to test in all of them, especially as it would probably have been developed to solve systems that have no analytical solution to check against. However, even for the most general of simulators it will be possible to test certain simple models that do have analytical solutions, e.g. the $M/D/1$.

12.2 ACCELERATED SIMULATION

In the discussion on random number generation we mentioned that the computing time required to simulate 10^{12} cells is impractical, although cell loss probabilities of 10^{-10} are typically specified for ATM buffers. In fact, most published simulation results for ATM extend no further than probabilities of 10^{-5} or so.

How can a simulation be accelerated in order to be able to measure such rare events? There are three main ways to achieve this: use more computing power, particularly in the form of parallel processing; use statistical techniques to make better use of the simulation measurements; and decompose the simulation model into connection, burst and cell scales and use only those time scales that are relevant to the study.

We will focus on the last approach because it extends the analytical understanding of the cell and burst scales that we developed in previous chapters and applies it to the process of simulation. In particular, burst scale queueing behaviour can be modelled by a technique called cell rate simulation.

Cell rate simulation

The basic unit of traffic with cell rate simulation is a "burst of cells". This is defined as a fixed cell rate lasting for a particular time period during which it is assumed that the inter-arrival times do not vary (see Figure 12.4). Thus instead of an event being the arrival or service of a cell, an event marks the change from one fixed cell rate to another. Hence traffic sources in a cell-rate simulator must produce a sequence of *bursts* of cells. Such traffic sources, based on a cell rate description have been covered in Chapter 4.

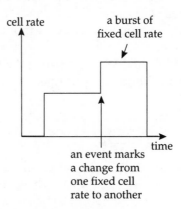

Figure 12.4
The basic unit of traffic in cell rate simulation

The multiplexing of bursts from different sources through an ATM buffer has to take into account the simultaneous nature of these bursts. Bursts from different sources will overlap in time and a change in the rate of just one source can affect the output rates of all the other VCs passing through the buffer.

An ATM buffer is described by two parameters: the maximum number of cells it can hold, i.e. its buffer capacity; and the constant rate at which cells are served, i.e. its cell service-rate. The state of a queue, at any moment in time, is determined by the combination of the input rates of all the VCs, the current size of the queue, and the queue parameter values.

The flow of traffic through a queue is described by input, output, queueing and loss rates (see Figure 12.5). Over any time period, all cells input to the buffer must be accounted for; they are either served, queued or lost. At any time, the rates for each VC, and for all VCs, must balance:

$$\text{input rate} = \text{output rate} + \text{queueing rate} + \text{loss rate}$$

When the queue is empty, the output rates of VCs are equal to their input rates, the total input rate is less than the service rate, and so there is no burst scale queueing.

$$\text{output rate} = \text{input rate}$$
$$\text{queueing rate} = \text{loss rate} = 0$$

In a real ATM system there will of course be cell scale queueing, but this behaviour is not modelled by cell rate simulation. When the combined input rate exceeds the service rate, the queue size begins to increase at a rate determined by the difference in the input rate and service rate of the queue.

$$\text{queueing rate} = \text{input rate} - \text{service rate}$$

For an individual VC, its share of the total queueing rate corresponds to its share of the total input rate. Once the queue becomes full, the total

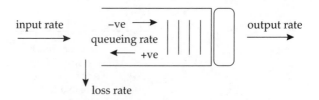

Figure 12.5
The balance of cell rates in the queueing model for cell rate simulation

queueing rate is zero and the loss rate is equal to the difference in the input rate and service rate.

$$\text{loss rate} = \text{input rate} - \text{service rate}$$

Although this appears to be a simple model for the combined cell rates, it is more complicated when individual VCs are considered. An input change to a full buffer, when the total input rate exceeds the service rate, has an impact not only on the loss rate but also on all the individual VC queueing rates. Also, the effect of a change to the input rate of a VC, i.e. an event at the input to the queue, is not immediately apparent on the output, if there are cells queued. At the time of the input event, only the queueing and/or loss rates change. The change appears on the output only after the cells which are currently in the queue have been served. Then at the time of this output event, the queueing and output rates change.

It is beyond the scope of this book to describe the cell rate simulation technique in more detail, however we present some results in Figure 12.6 which illustrate the accelerated nature of the technique. In comparison with cell by cell simulation, cell rate simulation shows significant speed increases, varying from 10 times to over 10 000 times faster. The speed improvement increases in proportion to the average number of cells in a fixed rate burst, and also increases the lower the utilisation and hence, also, the lower the cell loss. This is because it focuses processing effort on the traffic behaviour which dominates the cell loss: the burst scale queueing behaviour. So cell rate simulation enables the low cell loss probabilities required of ATM networks to be measured within reasonable computing times.

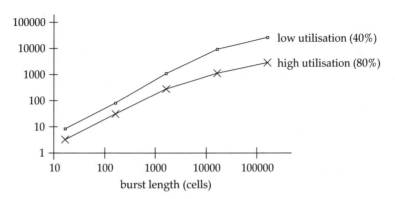

Figure 12.6
Speed increase of cell rate simulation relative to cell by cell simulation

References

[1] Griffiths, J.M. (ed.), *ISDN Explained: Worldwide Network and Applications Technology*, (John Wiley & Sons), ISBN 0471 93480 1 (1992)

[2] Cuthbert, L.G. and Sapanel, J-C., *ATM: the Telecommunications Network Solution*, (The Institution of Electrical Engineers), ISBN 0 85296 815 9 (1993)

[3] Law, A.M. and Kelton, W.D., *Simulation Modelling and Analysis*, (McGraw-Hill), ISBN 0 07 100803 9 (1991)

Index